MW01118135

Free Your Mind

131 Poems For Inner Peace

By Adam Oakley

COPYRIGHT

Text, Image and Cover Copyright © Adam Oakley 2015.

All Rights Reserved.

Adam Oakley asserts the moral right to be identified as the author of this work.

These poems are works of fiction. The names, characters and incidents portrayed within it are the work of the author's imagination. Any resemblance to actual persons, living or dead, events or localities is entirely coincidental and unintended.

By payment of the required fees, you have been granted the non-exclusive, non-transferable right to access and read the text of this book. No part of this book or text may be reproduced, transmitted, downloaded, decompiled, copied, reverse engineered, or stored in or introduced into any information storage and retrieval system, in any form or by any means, whether electronic or mechanical, now known or hereafter invented, without express written permission of the author Adam Oakley.

ISBN: 978-1-912720-39-2

www.InnerPeaceNow.com

www.AdamOakleyBooks.com

Published by Oakhouse Publications.

Oakhouse Publications

Contents

Introductory Lines

This entire book of poetry, has come as a surprise,
Suddenly these poems decided they all wanted to arise,
And so here they are in book form of considerable size,
Pointing to an intelligence that flows throughout our lives.

An intelligence that's natural, which is the same as Nature,
Some may call it God or Life, the Universe or Creator.
The intelligence that beats your heart, that regulates the breath,
The source of thought, the home that exists, that houses birth and death.

Whatever name you have for it, it makes itself announced,
As the existence that you are, the silence beneath the sounds,
Or the love you feel when for a moment you are free from lack or fear,
When you no longer have the deceitful voice that whispers in your ear.

It's scary to the mind that is addicted to its movements,
But is itself the ever-free abode beyond improvements.

An intelligence that unites us all, that man has just forgotten,
Turning a paradise of a world to reflect a mind that's rotten.
But rotting doesn't last forever, it's part of Nature's cycle,
As following the light of day comes the inevitable nightfall.

And after falling asleep for a while, now we can awake,
From a dream creating a world where so much food can
go to waste,
Or where more money is spent on war than is needed to
end all hunger,
A world where we make enemies of our sisters and our
brothers.

This book contains no answers, yet it contains no lies,
Words can point straight to truth, but they also can
disguise.
The truth is in between the words, in which the words
arise,
Focus on the words too much, and then the truth will
hide.

The heaven is within us, like that famous guy once said,
You don't have to wait for it until after you are dead.
What dies is the idea of yourself created in your head,
Formed of thoughts and memories making you feel
separate from the rest.

I do hope you enjoy the book, that it can enrich your life,
That the poems and the words can help to calm a restless
mind,
To take it back to its resting place that's also filled with
joy,
Where a struggling mentality need no longer be
employed.

With the capacity of humans, we can create a living hell,
But with a simple shift in consciousness we could do
rather well,
And create a world together that reflects our natural
state,
Where we no longer feel cut-off from an existence that is
great.

Enjoy it all, it's all a game, forget everything you know,
Disregard these words as well and life can truly flow.
Opened up to intelligence and creativity,
Life then uses you, so it can fulfill its destiny.

A Wild Bull

The effort to make the mind quiet,
Is like holding a wild bull on a leash.
The leash is held on to, and he drags you around,
And you are determined not to release.

One day maybe the bull will stop moving,
And finally you can rest.
Or you can stop expecting the bull to be still,
And let go of the leash, instead.

Once you don't care what the bull does,
When you no longer seek to control him,
Wherever he goes and whatever he does,
Does not affect the one watching.

A bull moves around, that's what it does,
If you fight him, he fights you back.
Don't ask the mind to be silent,
Then silence is all that you have.

The Swimming Mind

The struggling mind fights and moves,
Like someone swimming on top of the sea.
It desperately wants to find the route,
So it can rest and finally be free.

Someone calls out at the swimmer,
"Just drown and have it all done!"
The swimmer refuses to go deeper,
And waits till the rescue boat comes.

It waits and it waits, always it is waiting
For its saviour to come and to save it.
"Once the boat is here, then I can rest,
And my struggle will be old and outdated!"

But the boat never comes, and the swimmer keeps searching,
Wanting and hoping for release.
The mind grows exhausted and gives up its yearning,
And the swimmer is sucked down into the sea.

The swimmer does drown, it may have been painful,
It certainly wasn't what they expected.
And after they've gone, all that remains,
Is the depth of the sea, unaffected.

By Itself

A tree grows, your heart beats,
The wind blows, your lungs breathe.

It happens, by itself.

Thoughts come then disappear
As quickly as they came,
Disappearing by themselves,
Without a trace or name.

No-one is thinking, no-one is feeling,
No-one is breathing, no-one is eating.

It happens, by itself.

The Universe's Experience

Everything in experience has already appeared,
The universe is dancing.
If you try to manipulate the dance of experience,
You will feel trapped in a movement of suffering.

If you see that your experience is already allowed,
That the universe is letting it happen,
Then the person that tries to manipulate experience,
Dissolves back into the background.

It is the universe's burden, not yours or mine,
When thoughts and sensations arise.
So let the universe carry on as it wishes,
And dissolve the suffering mind.

Without Trying

A silence that doesn't try to be silent,
A Life that isn't trying to live.
A peace that houses all that arises,
An emptiness without any ideas.

Noise can flow in an untroubled space,
The space will not make a complaint.
Noise can complain that itself is too noisy,
While the silence has nothing to say.

The effortlessness of silence already,
Is the freedom so obvious and clear.
But believe you are merely the noises on top,
And you may be troubled for many a year.

Noise calls out in a heavenly silence,
Saying "One day I shall reach the great peace."
When all of this time, you are the being,
That sits quietly at peace, underneath.

A Useful Reminder

How useful it can be to realise
That no body will last forever.
Sounds depressing at first, but to real eyes,
It's like Nature is changing the weather.

When you no longer assume that all will last,
You no longer take them for granted -
The people in life that have always been there,
But one day will appear as departed.

Death is something we talk about,
But no one can really fathom.
But to accept the impermanence of human beings,
Will enlighten your interactions.

Anyone who makes you feel bad,
Will one day be dead in the grave.
And when your body expires,
You'll not give a damn what they say.

Knowing that humans aren't forever,
Decreases hatred and judgement.
And at the same time, for those who you love,
You'll appreciate them in abundance.

You won't get bogged down in the silly small things,
That often eat away inside.
The little but painful, niggles of life,
Are seen in the light, and subside.

Anyone you love, who is valued in life,
Will now be valued all the more.
Cherished, appreciated, not overlooked,
And yet not so clung to anymore.

We tend to assume that all is forever,
Then when someone dies we are surprised.
Don't wait for death to come and remind you
Who you really love in your life.

Looking at how the people all come
And go like a morning breeze,
You'll worry less, arguments will decrease,
And you'll marvel at all of the trees!

Guess

I am what the mind has invented.
Without the mind, do I even exist?
Without thought being at all implemented,
Does my reality within you persist?

I have the whole world in a great worry,
And to question my existence is taboo,
Since without me, no one can worry,
And so people would not know what to do.

Ask the animals of me, ask the trees and the Earth,
And they will not be too sure what you mean.
I am inserted in your head from the moment of birth,
And if I stay you can't really feel free.

Question my existence, scrutinise my worth,
And you may be in for a big surprise,
It will remove your fear of coffin and hearse,
When you realise there is no time.

The Pretender

I pretend to be helping people up, but I keep everybody down,
I pretend I will soon stop, but I keep going round and round,
I pretend to be the very thing that will take me away,
And then I keep on going, taking energy all day.

I pretend that I am them, and they are intimately me,
So if I was gotten rid of, extinguished they would also be.
How clever it is you see,
That I promote a problem and then offer to fix it for them,
Whilst they believe I am helping, I distract them from their boredom.

I am worthy to be trusted I do regularly assure them,
It is a must that they believe that I'm of course very important.

I am homeless but choose to stay with anyone who will have me,
Anyone who hates me or anyone who grabs me.
My eviction notice comes when I am seen as a useless guest,
My name is worry, and I promise that I wish you all the best.

<u>Watch Anything</u>

Watch anything, and it will teach you,
The illusory nature of time.
A tree, a bird, a clock, a chair,
Will all show the trick of the mind.

The clock that ticks, ticks only now,
It has no memories of when it has ticked.
The tree has no idea what time might be,
And the chair could not care one bit.

Ask a bird what time it is,
I tried once and it flew away.
Either it was scared of talking to me,
Or it would not give me the time of day.

Everything changes, so we say there is time,
And our memories prove it as fact.
If thought is not used, and simply we look,
Do we really go forward or back?

Life

Life doesn't need your help to get by,
It's quite fine all by itself.
It takes care of your breathing and heartbeat,
Your digestion and movements as well.

Declare that you are separate,
And the intelligence of Life is masked,
Worried and hurried or stopped and delayed,
Living for future or past.

Look outside and wonder,
How it's possible for you to be separate.
The universe is a unified whole,
And the separate self is vacant.

Infinite Space

A person travels above, through infinite space,
In their space suit, looking for something.
They look left and right, forward and back,
And they are spotted by someone who's watching.

"What is it you need?" someone calls after them,
As they look up to notice the person,
"I'm going on a search to find infinite space!"
Comes the reply shouted down with assertion.

"Stop and look around, you are already there,"
Comes the call from the quiet spectator.
"Leave me alone, I'm so nearly there!"
He will find the infinite later.

He goes on his search, travels for years,
Visiting all of the galaxies,
Never realising that his sought-after infinite space
Is the very space that he travels in.

Don't Be Lazy. Please.

Don't be lazy, don't just sit there.

You may realise you are the whole universe.

How can we control you if you are no longer scared?

How can we convince abundance that there is lack?

How can you fit in with the people, when you no longer even exist?

Quick, get up. Do something. Please.

A Period Of Laze

What can look to worldly eyes as a period of laze,
Can actually be an energy and pre-creation phase.

The fertile ground for new ideas and actions to all
sprout,
Where inspiration can be the food to let the freshness
out.

If you feel creative, do you make it so?
Or is it flowing from a force over which you have no
control?

And if you feel all stagnant, is this something to protest?
Or is it something not to judge, and let it let you rest?

We can get in such a mess when we think we know
what's best,
When you are a tool of Nature, who's in charge of birth
and death.

I don't mean just birth and death of body, I mean all the
rest –
Ideas, actions, results, attempts, situations and events.

And when you fight against her, this of course is stress.

Let go of what you think would really be so great,
And let Nature move in ways that you could never
predict as fate.

If that feels no good for you, if it doesn't resonate,
Then act as if you never read it, and have lovely day.

Creativity

A bursting forth of creation,
Flows swift through an empty mind.
A mind not forcing, but open,
To the force that can come any time.

Unannounced he comes, but call him,
And he may start to play hide and seek.
But let creativity use you when he wants,
And you are the tool he can then use with ease.

The Game Of Nearly There

Maybe we've been playing this game for thousands of years,
The game of "nearly there".
Perhaps it's something that's strung us along,
Like a con-man in your ear...

"That was great, now you're nearly there,
Nearly close to freedom,
Till then I'll hold your freedom hostage,
Unreleased till I have good reason."

Freedom on hold, release kept suspended,
Waiting for the 'next',
Then if the next thing comes along,
The whole game starts again.

<u>Melt</u>

What's right and what's wrong,
What's spiritual and what's not.
What's good and what's bad,
What's the best way to act.

All these things one is told,
Voices in the ears.
Some mean well, some may not,
But all opinions and ideas.

This voice says, the simple solution:
Stop fighting with yourself.
Don't say how you should feel or be,
And the useless stuff will melt.

By itself.

How Would It Feel?

How would it feel to not want anything?
To not want anything from your life?
To not feel as if you need anything else
To put an end to struggle and strife?

How would it feel to not believe
That your Life is not yet complete?
To feel as if there is nothing more
That you need to really be free?

How would it feel to make no demands?
To stop asking that Life should fulfill you?
To put end to complaint, and all the commands,
That may have earlier built you?

I'll leave it open, they are just questions
To explore within oneself,
To see if any of your mental discomforts
Actually give Life any help.

The Vacant Abode

The nothingness of sleep, the vacant abode,
We love to vanish into every night.
But the nothingness of death, that calls everyone,
Can give us a great deal of fright.

As soon as we wake we are told to be something,
We put on our names and labels.
Instead of bearing the weight of society's words,
Stay as nothing that words can resemble.

Spiritual Obsession

Spirituality can quickly become just another obsession,
Another thought-based accumulator of mental lessons,
Another thing or experience to achieve in the future,
That will then be a "perfect life" producer.

Maybe that's part of the game, but don't be a concept-slave.

Who is actually reading this? Where are the words landing?

Do they even land? Where do they go?

Who is at the bottom of this perception?

Who are you? Are you anything?

Everyone has told you that you are something.

Could they all be mistaken?

The Human Being

The human being is tiny,
But tends to want to play God,
Controlling life, manipulating things,
So things are the way that it wants.

From space, you can't even see human beings,
They are like ants on a faraway hill,
And yet we contend with the universe,
Saying all should conform to our will.

And so suffering ensues when Life decides
It will no longer meet expectations.
Living in life whilst clinging to it,
Can leave you feeling stuck in limitation.

If you give yourself up, don't try to play God,
Then maybe you'll be surprised,
When you no longer seek to grip on to the world,
It can't grip you on the inside.

If Energy Is Trapped

If energy is trapped,
It wants to be let out.
So if someone gets angry,
They feel they want to shout.

And if they feel in pain,
They want it out of them.
So easily if someone's hurting,
They'll even shout at friends,

Or family or loved ones that
They'd never like to hurt,
But when pain lives and is identified with,
It takes over someone's nerves,

And covers their eyes and rules their thoughts
So they can no longer see,
The pain that they are distributing
To those in their vicinity.

If this happens in you, just notice it,
Without trying to condemn.
And as you no longer interpret it,
Pain-spreading comes to an end.

And if you see it in others,
Who are apparently just rude,
You can notice they are trapped
In a mental servitude.

Perhaps even an illness,
Infected by a mind
That lives within and demonises
Everything inside.

If someone was possessed by something,
Or sleepwalking in the night,
And they insulted you or even
Tried to offer you a fight,
You may still act, even fight back
Who can predict such things?
But the difference would be you'd no longer take
Their actions personally.

It seems people have volition
Over what they think and feel,
Over how they act and what they say,
Be it stupid, fake or real.

But psychic energies influence,
Invisible to the eye.
It's still quite rare for a person
To be free from a painful mind.

But noticing things aren't so personal,
That people just react,
According to impulses that
Present their thoughts as facts -
It will no longer hit you so hard,
Or be kept inside your core.
And you'll not have to cling on to drama,
Because honestly, you'll be bored.

Interest keeps you stuck to things
That you may not wish to stick.
So lose interest in all the mess,
And you won't suffer a thing.

The G Word

If I mention God, I do not mean it to sound religious -
In terms of preachers and teachers lost in holy scriptures,
Believing in the words that have been twisted by people in a church,
Or a dogma that leads to conflict and other people being hurt.

What I mean by God, is the intelligence of Life,
You could call it Nature, Self, or something of that kind.
The Universe is a name that's used to point to the same thing,
But I'm aware that 'God' can make the inner alarm bells ring.

God is just the word I use that hits me in my heart,
But I don't take it as a man in the clouds, judging with a harp.
Without this force I wouldn't be able to breathe or even write,
Or speak or hear or read, or even experience this life.

The source that shines as the consciousness and unified light,
Whose home lies where you are, but completely out of sight.

Not a bloke who punishes, or tells people to fight,
Or who gives us all free will, then promotes destruction or delight,
By saying something like:
"Heaven's only where you go if you do what I say is right."

And at the same time, it's the origin of all religions,
That gets twisted by what's perhaps the definition of

some "sinners"
Who may "miss the mark", who do not seem to really
get the point,
Or who wish to fool the people, and only speak out
certain points…

The original pointings originally made by the original
masters,
Are usually not "religious", but are more like meditation
classes.
To keep quiet and sink in within, let your individuality
melt
In the very fire of the joy that is the Universal Self.

The definition of religion varies depending on who you
ask,
Some might call it man-made rules, to promote a ruling
class,
Others may call it just a stinking load of deluded arse,
Or some might say it has truth to it, but only in certain
parts.

What I call true religion, is to do with nothing that men
said.
Not to do with worshipping someone who's both alive
and dead,
But worshipping the very Life that creates all this
instead,
That can organise your life without carrying the weight
on your own head.

Until the thing that's worshiped swallows up the one
who worships,
The force that flows through Nature, in the ground and
in the turnips,
And the food and drink and air to breathe that constitutes
your body,

Which is the fibre of everything once our minds drop all their stories.

But all in all, the apparent arrogance to act as if one understands,
An unknowable divinity with or without an untold plan,
Is like a child counting a few grains while they are sitting in the sand,
And saying "I know how many grains that there are in all the land!"

Hopefully you catch my drift, and I have made my point,
So hopefully if I use the G-word, it will not disappoint.
And to those who are religious, I do not wish to offend,
Surely all the sacred figures, were God disguised as men.

What Is It About Death?

What is it about death that can be so scary?
Perhaps it's the loss of control.
In the world it seems you can control what you do,
But death makes you let all of that go.

We can make plans for where we will be in five years,
Like our destiny is in our hands.
But the moment the body goes back to the Earth,
Is probably not in your plans.

The illusion is that you can pick or choose,
That the world is in your personal power.
But dying destroys the entire illusion,
And forces you to retire.

Perhaps it exposes our arrogance,
Of believing that we control life.
We have a few years, a few million breaths,
Then death comes to end all our strife.

So many things seem under control,
We can manage them, hold them together,
Ignoring and scared that our very own deaths,
Can not be controlled or made better.

It requires letting go, a surrender to life,
Of realising you can no longer fight.
When death comes along, in the day or the night,
Letting your burdens all burn in the light.

Perhaps it is like playing outside as a child,
Running in the rain and the wind.
The parents call you to come back home where it's safe,
But you refuse to want to go in.

The feeling of being an individual,
A person with autonomy,
Gets destroyed by something called death that seems
To happen to all that we see.

You can't keep your old identity alive
If you lose possession of your body,
No more me, no more you,
No more collection of stories.

Straight after birth, the identity comes,
An identity you are told to hold dear.
What does death do but remove the self
That was purely made up of ideas?

An idea of self, everybody is trained
To hold on to, keep and protect.
For the first time in life, perhaps it scares
To not have a clue what comes next.

But this is all gibberish, mere speculation,
Discussing what can't be discussed.
After writing a piece of writing like this,
I just feel like shutting the f**k up.

Just Keep Thinking

Entangled in understanding,
Trapped in its own security,
Searching for relief from its own energy,
A movement of thought goes on relentlessly.

One day you can understand all of this.
One day you will know all of the answers.

Just. Keep. Thinking.

Then you can fix your problems,
Then you can rest from the world and be at peace.

But first, keep thinking.

Whatever you do, don't give up your concepts,
Do not relinquish your life to the power that keeps your
heart beating.
Hold on to your separateness, feel alone so that one day
you may conquer life.

Just. Keep. Thinking.

The Doer Ship

All aboard the Doer Ship,
Where doership is a must.
The ship fills up, with people who trust
That their efforts are an absolute must.

They sail on the ship, it has no engine,
No sails to catch the breeze.
Instead the ship relies solely on,
The waves and movement of sea.

The ship sails around, miraculously,
Out of the harbour and back.
Each of the passengers enjoy their ride,
Then after they say, "Look. I did that!"

"That was my doing! I made those waves,
I got us through the excursion."
Rarely do ever the passengers notice,
The sea took all of the burden.

If You Want To Be Unhappy...

If you want to be unhappy,
Make sure you do these five things.
The first is to control people,
Especially what they think.

The second is to fight life,
To complain and judge against it.
The third is to wish that
Others should give you acceptance.

The fourth is to believe that
Every thought must be true.
The fifth is to take the burden of life,
And believe what happens is up to you.

But if any of that makes you happy,
Throw these words into the wind.
And then in either case it may be clear,
Where happiness really lives.

"I Can't Stop Thinking"

"I can't stop thinking", because "I" *is* thinking,
If "I" starts to stop thinking, it feels it is sinking.
When it feels it is sinking, it can not survive,
So it would rather cause trouble, than give up its life.
But it has become silly, it just causes trouble,
Makes a mess of itself and causes a muddle,
It curses up at the rain, then steps in a puddle.

The thinking is no longer helping.

He talks all day, gives some advice,
He pretends to be bad, pretends to be nice.

But still he won't shut up.

If he's told to shut up, he probably won't,
Like a friend become rigid and stubborn.
He's boring, give him the silent treatment,
And he will vanish, all of a sudden.

Let The World Breathe

What are you doing up there, on the surface of things,
Where you get battered and bruised, so easily?
Why is it you are addicted to these,
Disturbances that take your energy?

You're told it's your job, to manage the world,
To be in charge of your life.
To make sure it all doesn't collapse,
And be left with nothing that's right.

Since of course all will go wrong if you let go your grip,
If you let go of the hold on the world.
But the world wants to breathe, and once you let go,
You can stop exerting yourself.

And when the world breathes it gives you release,
You let go of it, it lets go of you.
The bondage is there when the tight gripping hand
Dominates the entire worldview.

Let the world breathe, let Nature be free,
It removes all your burden and weight.
A wise man once said that the world's made of rings,
You only need make your own hooks straight.

He Is Mysterious

He is mysterious, but he is ever-present,
Like the air that I breathe but cannot see.
She takes care but I do not understand her,
And it has taken my responsibility.

I know not, for a fact, anything.
How these words come, I can not say.
And yet they emerge, on to the page,
Like the sunlight appears in the day.

Whatever I think about him deceives me,
Whatever I say about her is a lie,
It creates this experience, sustains me, perceives me,
And it is what will remain when I die.

How all of this happened, I do not know,
He is a mysterious thing.
But she has no shape, no form of which to speak,
It is silent, but loves to sing.

The power sustaining life emanates from his core,
But without her even knowing.
Its ultimate place is beyond even Life,
From where everything else is outflowing.

Criticism

Whatever you do or do not do,
Praise and criticism are likely.
It is extremely rare that anyone does anything,
And there are *only* people that like it.

Don't act, then someone may criticise,
Saying you were too scared or too lazy.
Do act, and someone else may pipe up,
Saying you were reckless or crazy.

Criticism is for work or action,
It is not actually about you.
And criticism can be extremely helpful,
If the advice is useful and true.

We are taught we should avoid criticism,
That it is bad and praise is good,
So we hunt for the praise and avoid all the pain,
That we think criticism hides under its hood.

But criticism from the wise develops your craft,
And if it is useless it will mean nothing at all.
Don't try to avoid the unavoidable,
And you will rise up rather than fall.

Praise and criticism are both unavoidable,
They are there wherever you turn.
So you can stop trying to avoid what can't be escaped,
And let yourself develop and learn.

Cleared And Cleaned

Clouded eyes are cleared by the wind,
That flows like the breath of the universe,
That blows out all of the useless hurts,
And whispers without mentioning a word.

Then the vision is clear, and all is pristine,
The eyes aren't deciding what's what,
The mind can't understand a lot,
And it leaves an undisturbed scene.

Everything starts to glisten and gleam,
The world looks strangely serene,
The universe vibrates within the Supreme,
A clouded vision is cleaned.

Before Words

Before the words arise,
Before "I" or even "I Am",
What is there that exists without
The idea of a woman or man?

Before all the stories, all the ideas
Of who you are or what you did.
Before we talk of a future self,
Before we describe what the world is.

Who is there? Is anybody there?
Who are you before all the words?
What is the existence, prior to all,
Within which even existence is heard?

We sleep, then we dream, then we wake then we sleep,
A cycle that seems quite complete.
But who or what do these things rotate in,
And yet does not move along with the scenes?

An unmovable, untouchable, unfathomable,
Unknowable, wordless reality.
Words are mere paupers trying to describe
The unimaginable majesty.

Don't Bother

Don't bother fixing it for a moment,
Just let it be.
Give it some room, give it some space,
Give it some air to breathe.

Don't jump on its back just yet,
Or it will carry you all over the place.
If you want to eliminate or beat it,
You'll end up in a war or a race.

It may have gone by now, it was just passing through,
It was never yours in the first place.
Never your problem, not yours to fix,
Relax, you're not in the workplace.

Supreme Laziness

The supreme laziness,
Is to not bother about yourself.
To not take interest in what your mind says,
To disregard what does not come to help.

To let all come and go, without caring an inch,
About what even you may think.
No longer interested in approaching all things,
With the intention of always to fix.

Trouble in your mind?
Don't bother about it.

Seeking but can't find?
Don't bother about it.

Noise disturbs silence?
Don't bother about it.

Discomfort is inside?
Don't bother about it.

Problems in your head?
Don't bother about them.

Worrying in your bed?
Don't bother about it.

Not yet "enlightened"?
Don't bother about it.

Perhaps you are frightened?
Don't bother about it.

Can't calm down?

Don't bother about it.

Feel your whole world is upside-down?
Don't bother about it.

Annoyed? In joy? Frustrated? Elated? Perfect?
Imperfect? Abundant? Redundant?
Don't bother about it.

This, is supreme laziness.

Then the Supreme moves you.

God's Peace

The only peace is God's peace,
So I give it back to him.
I'll stop trying to create it myself,
And stop trying to take it from him.

I've talked over God, I've got in the habit,
Of demanding my desires be met.
And whilst I don't shut up, I speak over the one,
And take my burdens on my own head.

The one without which I couldn't perceive,
I couldn't feel, I couldn't breathe,
I couldn't see, my heart would not beat,
And he seems to do it with ease.

Dissolve me in your presence,
Stop letting me be so deluded.
My final demand, and let it now end,
So that all of this mess can be through with.

The Separation

The separation between the world and me,
"I am looking at things from inside my body".
The seer is separated from the seen,
You are inside the head, looking out at a scene.

The "I" says it looks out from behind the eyes,
Search it out, expose its disguise.
Dressed in sensation, you may be surprised,
To not find yourself as a thing.

Where does "I" live, from where do you see?
Are you a self? Are you a "me"?
Is there perhaps a possibility
That "you" don't even exist?

That the self, perhaps is a myth?
That looking for yourself you can't find it?
That whatever you point to, whatever it is,
Is like the ocean thinking it must be a fish?

The observer seems separate from the observed,
To dispute this statement seems almost absurd.
The hearer seems separate from the heard,
Always the self wants to make its escape.

Pull itself away, give itself shape,
Recoil from what rises and falls,
And form a relationship on duality laws,
To say what it loves and say what it hates.

As you look out at the world,
Where does the world end and you begin?
The one that claims to see the world,
Is this person even a real thing?

Find the line, the point of distinction,
Between the seer and all it can see.
You're told that you are a separate thing,
But you are God, and this is a dream.

Original Consumers

A young group of people started their training
In a beautiful paradise of a place.
The food was bountiful, the water was pure,
And the houses they lived in were great.
They had everything and more, abundantly rich,
And as their training began,
They all gathered round the large golden table,
And the trainers unfolded their plan.

The children sat down, listened and wrote,
Their diamond pens dancing and glistening.
They concentrated hard, paid great attention,
As they were taught to see only what's missing.
Lack was the aim, not enough was the tool,
To get them to always want more,
Gifts all day the children were given,
And they reported on how they fell short.

"Not quite sweet enough", or "Should be more sweet",
"Not enough of these", or "Too many".
As long as they described something not right,
Then their marks and grades would stay steady.
They got more creative, more and more skilled,
At seeing the wrong or the missing,
When given good food, perfect on plate,
They decided it arrived far too quickly.

And as they became more and more glum
At how they had nothing they wanted,
They traipsed around their paradise of an island,
Feeling quite lost and despondent.
The overflowing riches that brimmed all around them
Were overlooked and no longer seen.
The first needy batch of human consumers,
Were now ready for their timely release.

They moved out in the world, spread like a disease,
Infecting all of those they would meet.
They convinced the whole world there wasn't enough,
And they needed much more before peace.
Resources were hoarded whilst more things were
bought,
They turned their world into a mess,
Enough for the whole world many times over,
But it seemed like there was now so much less.

All apart from the very small group
Who had trained the first batch of consumers.
The trainers by now where far richer than ever,
From people's belief in their horrible rumours.
They owned all the companies, that offered relief
From the life now full of toil and such lack.
Whilst selling them goods and employing the people,
Staff's wages they would soon get back.

They developed their countries, printed their money,
Still had enough to take care of them all,
But spent most of their money on fighting each other,
To get even more while others grew poor.
People were starving, others were fed,
From the masses of food that they had,
Whilst off out at sea they dumped tonnes of food,
To keep the food prices on track.

"It's how the world is. There isn't enough",
The trainers would say to trainees,
Whilst in the evening off they would go,
To rest in their mansions at ease.
If the people would question: "Is it the case
That there really isn't enough?
Or have we been duped, and there is plenty,
And life need not be so tough?"

Then perhaps they would see, that their world provides plenty,
That the problem mostly does lie,
In the mindset of man, his greed and his fear,
And his tendency to tell lies.
That the society they build, take part in and sustain,
Reflects the beliefs of the people,
That each must first address his or her mind,
And dig up the root of their evil.

Beware of deceit, beware of corruption,
Not only from your fellow man,
But the voice in your head that causes you pain,
And leaks out into the land.
If the mind is in turmoil, then so is the world,
The two are one and the same.
The world can shift to a healthier place,
When the mind is no longer insane.

Fine

Fine, there is no line,
Between the seer and all that is seen,
These words come from no one, and fortunately,
No one is left to be free.

What If, 1

What if it were all a lie,
Your name, your age, the idea that you'll die,
What if it were all a lie?

You are given your name, you are told your age,
But who were you before this?
Your body has changed and so has your age,
But you've been here, and you saw this.

The personality you think you may have,
Will be different in another five years.
Everything changes, pops up then leaves,
Arises then disappears.

But something is changeless, who is he?
Who is the changeless one?
The one without name, gender or age,
Who was there before meeting your mum?

A self made of stories, are the stories true?
Or are they just make-believe?
Constructs of thought that fall away
As easily as autumn leaves?

What if you are born into a world
Where everyone thinks they know what they're doing?
They think they understand what the world is,
How life works, what's a bad or a good thing.

They teach you to live, tell you the rules
Of how the whole massive thing works.
Then a while later you suddenly realise
That most of your teachers were berks.

Fools who meant the best they could,

But limited all the same,
By their own upbringings, limited minds,
And a voice in the head that's insane,
Who is so quick to praise or blame,
Or can never admit a mistake,
Who has not a clue what is really going on,
Like a driver thinking the clutch is the brake.

A baby is born in an insane asylum,
The patients teach it what's right.
It leaves when it's older, and its whole mental world
Is exposed as a bunch of lies.

What If, 2

What if none of it is true?
That what is real can't be seen, and what is perceived,
Is as real as a white ninja flute.

What if your name isn't you?
That it's just like a label that you stick on the fridge,
And soon it will be chucked down the chute?

What if your age isn't true?
That it's just a concept of man to understand things,
But has nothing to do with you?

What if your thoughts are a lie?
Thieves in disguise, who wriggle and fight,
Trying to get food in the night?

What if your own opinions,
Seem to be your own things,
As if you made them, but really they are
Like birds flying over the sea?

What if the world is just like a dream?
When it's there it seems so real,
Then as soon as you wake, you forget what took place,
Your attention it no longer steals.

The Treasure Room

Climbing up, straining and efforting,
Reaching the door to the riches above.
Four steps gone, one more left,
He is determined not to give up.

He reaches the door, opens it up
And finds an empty room.
He turns around to look down the stairs,
And has struggled out of a golden tomb.

His riches were where he began from,
He had not to do a thing,
But it took him so long to climb up the stairs,
He does not want to go back to beginning.

So he stays up with effort, resisting,
Yearning for treasure but staying upstairs,
He can't bring himself to walk back down,
So frustrated he grabs at his hair.

Luckily the whole stairway gives way
When it no longer can take his weight.
He returns to his original glory,
Engulfed by the richness that always awaits.

Give Up The Rebellion

Simply give up the rebellion,
The rebellion against Life as it is.
Life flows and then an energy within
Says "no it should not be like this".

This is the main cause of suffering,
Of dictating how Life should be.
Appearances rise and fall like the sea,
But ego wants to control all that it sees.

Life is already moving,
It doesn't need any more help.
When you stop believing you know better than Life,
Suffering can no longer dwell.

Earth

A living being gives birth,
From itself it gives life and extends.
The planet that we call Earth,
That is the home of women and men.

The humans walk around as Earth's extensions
Being able to experience itself.
But with time come the human convictions
That they each have a separate self.

So all being one, all made of the same,
The humans declare they are separate.
They give too much importance to their labels and names,
And they divorce their marriage from Nature.

They walk around sick, incomplete,
Thinking they own the Earth.
Forgetting that without the Earth in the first place,
There would be neither death nor birth.

Their absolute reliance on Nature,
Is masked by the invention of money.
Which does have its place, but becomes absurd,
If no money means you'll go hungry.

Maybe they'll soon, together as one,
See their inseparability from the Gaia.
A unity which puts an end to the human
Life of suffering and fear.

An Itch

Something must be able to stop it,
The itching in my brain.
The itch that is never scratched for long,
And easily complains.

The itch that exists in the core of the mind,
That is searching for relief,
Not knowing it is itself the cause,
For its own misery and grief.

Facebook, Twitter, the next social media,
The TV, films and the games,
These things at my fingers like artificial nails,
And yet the itch in my brain still remains.

No more scratching, no more fixing,
No more asking the world to relieve it.
If the itch can't be scratched by anything outside it,
Then I will stop even trying to ease it.

The itch had been the looking in the first place,
Demanding the world give me peace.
But asking the changeful to give you rest,
Is like demanding your heart not to beat.

It doesn't make sense, it goes against nature,
The forms are not where my rest lies.
Until it is seen we are beyond all of these,
The itching can't wither and die.

Then the world is spirit's disguise.

The Foundation

A little man stands atop a giant foundation,
Resting on the ground of God.
He looks all around and with no hesitation,
Refuses to come down from the top.

The rain comes, the wind blows,
God calls a storm to knock him off,
Since within the foundation is a beautiful cove,
Where the man will never grow old.

"Get back inside you silly old fool!"
God shouts at the man who's still standing.
"No!" he replies, "I like it outside,
From here I feel tall and commanding."

The storm gets worse and the man holds on,
Being violently blown by the wind.
"I will not budge, it's Me vs God
And I will never go in!"

He stays out there for painful years,
Then decides he must find his shelter.
He searches the place for the entry point
To escape from God's turbulent weather.

"Take me in God, now I am ready,
Where is the door? I can't find it!"
"You have to shut up and stop moving" God says,
"And I'll make this your final retirement."

But the man doesn't stop moving, he wants the
achievement
Of being accepted into God's house.
The ground will swallow him up if only he gives up,
His efforts to control his own self.

And so he must wait till he physically dies,
He could not surrender before.
And once the breath of life leaves him,
He no longer wants anything more.

The ground engulfs him, swallows him whole,
As if the man never existed.
His struggle is over, his battle with Life
Is finally and gladly relinquished.

Orchestration

Give up your orchestration,
Aren't you tired by now?
A person pretending to conduct the music,
While the speakers are playing it loud.

Orchestrating thoughts, people, events,
Deciding how all should be,
Then trying to fix it all in place,
So your mind can be put at ease.

Do you even decide what your next thought should be?
Can you predict, have you any idea?
The moment you predict what you will think of next,
A thought has already appeared.

Do you decide your mood, bad or good?
Do you tell people to act a certain way?
Or is it the life responding to itself,
And it is more of an energetical game?

If you control something in the first place,
Then maybe it is yours to hold.
But if the whole world has appeared without your consent,
Then how can it be in your control?

I don't know, maybe it is,
These words are completely random.
Or were they destined to come out like this
And bring about this whole interaction?

I don't know, I'll leave it at that,
I don't know what other nonsense I'll say,
Trying to describe the nature of things,
Giving an invisible being a name.

The Imposter

An energy takes refuge inside the head,
It says, *"Yes, this will be my home.*
I shall turn the unity of Nature
Into something to call my own.

I shall split things up, imagine events,
I shall store up memories,
Then project these events as if yet to come
And call it the future, how heavenly.

I claim to live behind your eyes,
I separate myself from all that is seen.
The people, the things, the entire world,
I proclaim are all separate from me.

When thoughts come I treat them the same,
And I will say that I am the thinker.
Once again creating a separation,
Not letting attention go deeper.

I am the watcher, I am the 'me',
Separate from all other things.
I pretend to be the immutable one,
Who is one with all that it sees."

Stillness And Movement

Life consists of stillness and movements,
A flow of an unmoving space.
Demand that only stillness remains,
And the world will feel a turbulent place.

A mind will move and body will flow,
Don't interrupt with their movements.
If you interfere with the flow of the Life,
It may leave no room for improvements.

Stillness houses every movement,
That is its very magnificence.
It doesn't complain when it dances,
It is lost in its own brilliance.

Who is complaining, who is suffering,
When movement and sensations arise?
Discover this one, go to their root,
And there may be a pleasant surprise.

Let It Come Out

Let it come out,
That pain that's been inside for so long,
Let it come out,
Let the scream turn into a song.

Let it emerge out of your being,
By not arguing against it.
Let it flow in freedom,
Without trying to prevent it.

Or let it stick, if that's what it is doing,
But what is it sticking to?
It must be stuck to something else,
And is that something else really you?

Allow It

Allow that vulnerability you feel
That may shake your surface or core.
Don't try to hide it, don't try to mask it,
Just don't bother any more.

It is the prisoner inside wishing to come out,
Let them shake and tremble.
Once they break out, they will be free
And will dissolve and disassemble.

Everyone feels it, the vulnerable sense,
The fear of being destroyed.
Or of losing something that is held so dear,
Or of disappearing into the void.

If you cover it up, the shakiness stays,
Lurking under your layers.
Let it cry out and shake the place up,
Let the silence be your prayer.

Something Or Nothing?

Something can always happen to something,
Nothing can happen to nothing.
In a world of something that's made of nothing,
Will you be something or nothing?

Someone or no-one, a person or presence?
An object or the great abyss?
The objects that flow and flux in Life,
Or the home that is emptiness?

Make your stand in the changeful,
And you will be fighting the winds.
Dissolve back into the formless,
And you house all that is.

The house that contains all that is created,
And also all that is destroyed.
It makes perfect sense, you were there during birth,
And during death you will probably enjoy
A release from a world, collapsing back into God,
The home that we wished to escape,
The home where you can no longer control your own
life,
Or say whether you're bad or you're great.

Something or nothing, which are you?
Are you even beyond the two?
We talk about something, we talk about nothing,
And the one who knows them, is you.

My Role

The turbulence is unbearable,
I wish to be out of this mess.
Things shaking around me, completely unstable,
And I fear my destruction is next.

I look for refuge amongst the moving,
Everything trembles and creaks.
The instability of the world I see,
Leaves me feeling a constant unease.

Until I give up my search,
And call out, "Ok please!
I've had enough of all this, my plan didn't work."
And I'm forced down on to my knees.

God doesn't answer, and I get annoyed,
Why can't he make it more clear?
And then without speaking, he reveals it,
That I must first disappear.

How do I do that, how can I make
Myself disappear to make room
For God of all things surely its not up to me,
And the power all lies with you?

Why should I bear my own burden,
If the Lord sits right in my heart?
If it's true he is really running the show
Then why am I left in the dark?

Can't he take care of my part?
Is he really just having a laugh?
Is this all just some stupid illusion?
Are you really so distant and far?

All of the words disappear in the silence,
The same place from where they emerged.
The complainer, the crier, who's desperately tired,
Can no longer utter a word.

The lights go on, the stage is revealed,
I've taken a role inside of a play.
And I've been performing this desperate role,
Forgetting it was just to entertain.

And all of the pain, the desperate wish,
To be free from a world that's collapsing,
Has been from taking my role to be real,
When really it's all been God acting.

Pain And Pleasure

What is the difference between pleasure and pain,
At what point does pain become pleasure?
Or when does pleasure become pain?
Where is the mark that keeps them from being together?

If someone gently stroked your arm,
It might be rather pleasant,
But if they stroked it hard and with their nails,
Then that would be the end of the pleasure.

Someone gives you a hug,
It feels all warm and cosy,
But they start to squeeze harder, they cut off your air,
And your cheeks begin to go rosy.

The sweet taste of sugar, no doubt to many
– This is a form of pleasure.
Magnify it by one thousand and the discomfort it creates,
Would become a pain beyond measure.

A cold winter's night, you sit outside,
Warm by a burning fire.
But if you got closer, or went and sat in it,
To get away would be your only desire.

Is it that, perhaps, in fact,
Pain and pleasure are one and the same?
That pleasure is at one end of the scale,
Magnify it and then it's called pain?

If pain is there, treat it as pleasure.
Override your initial resistance.
Treat your pain as if you wish it were there,
And it may go into remission.

Or at least the relationship will change,
You will no longer struggle to avoid it.
Treat pain as pleasure, as if you want more,
And an embrace of love will then hold it.

Body Is A Temple

"My body is a temple" does not just mean you look after it.
It means God lives in it.
You go to the temple to worship the divine,
And the body is the walking temple.

Disappear in the temple, don't clutter up the place.
Don't go on filling noise in the embodiment of grace.
Go there and stay, since it contains all you need.
The worshipper dissolves, and what remains is free.

Spiritual Trap

Don't fall in to the spiritual trap
Of trying to feel a certain way.
All sensations thoughts, desires,
Arise in Nature's untouched space.

Surrendering to this
Then opens you to grace,
So the idea of 'you' diminishes,
And the pure Life takes its place.

Experiences are transient,
Some unpleasant, some are great.
But if we take away these names
Then is this really the case?

Without interpreting at all,
Then what really remains?
An unnamed, unknown,
Nothingness of space.

If we withhold opinions
Of what experience means,
Of which is a good or a bad one,
Or which one is best for peace,

No longer striving for an ease,
It is easier to see,
That there is no one suffering
Or bearing responsibility.

That without your judgments,
Experience has no reality.
The experiencer and experienced,
Dissolve like salt in sea.

That Nature bears the burden,
For what appears and disappears,
Not conflicting with experience,
Be it grief or joy or fear.

Then there is no one left
To be rebelling against life.
The dark contracted energy of "me"
By itself dissolves in light.

The Silent Abode

A bottomless silence that has no end,
Surely nothing can touch it.
Pain can't reach it, neither can pleasure,
It is exempt from destruction.

The home of all creation,
The source of Life, without trouble or fear.
Let the mind go home to the silent abode,
Without which nothing else would appear.

The silent abode where no-one lives,
If something is there, I can't say his name.
He has no form, he has no shape,
He doesn't care for your mistakes.

Always calling the mind back,
To where there is no more pain.
The end of the sense of being alone,
But still able to play in the game.

Take Up The Rebellion

Simply take up the rebellion
Of no longer conforming to things.
When voices call from inside and out,
No longer give them belief.

Words are like beautiful birds,
Let them fly in their majesty.
But if you grab hold of one as it flies,
It will peck at you with its beak.

Rebel, by no longer rebelling,
Win life by letting it go.
Don't cling to the illusory noises we make,
Then the freedom within will be known.

Or rather the one that is always trying to cover it up,
Dissolves back into its source.
Without taking the voices of the world to be true,
The rebellion has completed its course.

Everyone wants to give you
Their version of the world and things,
How things are and how things should be
And the way of the world as they see.

Each model of the world wants to be sustained,
Like an animal maintaining survival.
Even these words will carry a message,
Which you can throw out into the fire.

Where are you without the words?
Who have you ever been?
An answerless answer may be there,
The one who sees cannot be seen.

The Light Of The World

It's crazy how a figure like Jesus,
Is depicted as a perfect white man.
When really based on where he was born,
His skin would be much darker and tanned.

But it's easy to believe he was caucasian,
When that's all you grow up to see.
Ridiculous though, when obviously,
He was not European, but Asian.

Another thing with this famous guy,
Whose existence I don't argue with,
Is how he's presented as "meek and mild",
Is this pushover image a myth?

What about that story,
When he goes into the temple,

And sees the men using it as a market?

He loses his cool, goes completely berserk,
Throwing over tables and whipping the bastards.

But obviously, I have not a clue
Which stories are false and which are true.
Used as a tool to control the people,
The Bible's been altered by more than a few.

The wisdom of the philosopher Alan Watts,
And his knowledge of the scripture,
Pointed out a revelation to me,
That has been left out of the picture:

That when Jesus supposedly said to men
Opposing him in the scene,

That he was 'the' son of God,
With the crucial word being 'the' -
His original words actually read,
"Why do you say I blaspheme
when I say I am 'A' son of God"
Saying 'a' instead of 'the'.

And that 'a son' being changed to 'the son'
Was an error in translation,
A mistake that has wrongly influenced,
The mindsets of many nations.

And that in Hebrew "son of" is not literal,
But it means "the nature of",
As to call someone "a son of a *bitch*"
Does not imply their mother was a dog.

Doesn't that change the meaning considerably?
Completely turn religion on its head?
Fitting in with the account that he also
Reminded "thee are Gods" to the men?

And said that all the works he did,
We would do the same, and greater.
He might sound like the original evangelical preacher,
But I think we may have grossly misunderstood
The original message he was trying to teach us.

"The kingdom of heaven is within you",
I can not find a single line,
Where Jesus has said that heaven is a place
You go to when you die.

But I get what it means in a metaphorical way,
That the death is for "you" as an ego.
And that heaven is left as the reality that shines
When the mind isn't running the show.

Everything he said was a parable,
He spoke using stories and symbols.
So the returning of Christ might not be of Jesus,
But the spirit that spoke through the man to the people.

Whenever you read his words,
Read like he is speaking as spirit.
Then it all makes far more sense,
And his message has no arrogance in it.

"I am the way the truth and the life",
He is speaking from the essence of Christ.
Which was not only limited to a single man,
He said it was in all of us, right?

And that we are also the light?

"No man cometh unto the Father, but by me."
I don't think he was promoting himself.
He speaks as the eternal "I Am", existence.
The true nature of everyone's Self.

"Whatsoever ye shall ask the father in my name,
he will give it to you",
Did he mean his earthly name,
Or the "I Am" of which he, the man was a tool?

A realised being, one with all,
Full of devotion to the Father,
Came to renounce the common religions,
But is portrayed as religion's own matyr.

It's funny that a whole religion
Was built upon this man.
When whilst he was here he criticised
The religions and their plans.

And then there's the crucifixion,
Was it a literal story?
Or was it yet another parable,
Showing what comes when you give God your story?

When he says "Thy will be done",
He relinquishes all his resistance.
He gives up his will and replaces it with God's,
And he's swallowed up by the timeless existence.

"Jesus came to take away our sins",
Is this a literal statement? Was this a literal job?
Is he supposed to have taken our sins on the cross,
Or did he just show us, the way to God?

Religion

There is no doubt that religion
Has a beautiful side.
Once a Christian group prayed for me,
And right before my eyes,

I witnessed my own leg extend,
From its present size,
And extend an inch to match the other,
So that my hips were realigned.

And that is God's honest truth,
There was no cheat or trick,
It was on my very own leg,
And on another who came to sit.

But beware of course that religion,
Comes from the mind of man.
That God and religion,
Are not always hand in hand.

That religion can reflect,
The insanity of man,
Or can be used to control people,
To abide by human plans.

No doubt there is a power,
That flows through the universe.
It seems that all the great ones said,
To look within yourself, first.

The supreme that is not separate
From the nothing and the things,
The original message seems to be,
That within you, there is He.

And that He is not just limited
To only one body and mind,
But is the power and impersonal,
Existence and source of Life.

Let Death Come

Let death come for you.
It is ok, let yourself die in the Now.
Die to the past, die to the pain,
And die to the memories foul.

All of your past has disappeared,
It is not your job to keep it.
You don't have to correct what has disappeared,
Or caress, protect or believe it.

Perhaps many of us think our past should be perfect,
And to replay it might mean it will fix.
But all that holding on to events will do,
Is keep you feeling like you're stuck in some s**t.

It's not your job to correct what's gone,
Or even correct your own life.
You took this whole burden, only when you,
Were told that to bear burdens was right.

Give it back to the same force that created your body,
Without your mum choosing how you would form.
The power that continues the heart to beat,
Without which no one would even be born.

You may disagree, but you may well see,
That life is not your responsibility.
That the same force that brought you in to this world,
Will also take you out of the scene.

Death is not just for the physical,
It is when the mind realises its source.
That an intelligence lives, organising your life,
That exists even prior to thoughts.

Die into it, give yourself up,
Let it take "you" in.
The death can occur but the body can live,
And the spirit can fully move in.

The Most Joyful Man In The World

The most joyful man in the world,
Was absolutely crazy.
Whatever happened to him in his life,
You'd never catch him complaining.

You'd never hear him say anything
About something being wrong,
And so happy he was that sometimes he
Could not help but break into song.

"But man," they would say, *"aren't you annoyed*
That people have been saying bad things?
Saying that you are a terrible man,
And saying you really can't sing?"

"No," he would say, "I'm not annoyed,
I am ever so happy,
Because I throw my cares to the wind
And trust that Life will take care of me."

He skipped down the roads, ran on the fields,
Jumping in joy ever higher,
Because he treated all that arose
As if it were his very desire.

He never proclaimed that he wanted or wished
For something else to happen,
And so he was perfectly in line with his life,
And so were his interactions.

"Of course I want this to happen," he'd say,
"Why would I argue with Life?"
If I need to act, Life moves me,
And the responsibility is no longer mine.

"Life creates things, then sorts them out,
Why should I get stuck in the middle,
Proclaiming what's good or what shouldn't be happening,
Entangled in a difficult riddle?"

"Don't you get angry, or ever upset?"
"Yes I do from time to time.
But if that happens, I have no regret,
Since this is perfectly fine.

"In the same way I do not argue with things,
I do not conflict with my self.
Emotions can come and go as they like,
I will not resist them as well.

"So if anger is there I say 'hello my friend,
How lovely it is to see you,'
And whenever I do, he does not stay,
He says he must see other people.

"Misery comes, looking all glum,
I treat him as my chum.
He holds on my head for a little while then
He can't take my surrender, so runs.

"Nothing can happen unless Life says so,
I let Life take care of itself.
Some force created all this, to take it all on myself,
Would be very bad for my health!

"Everything I have, I want it,
Everything that comes, I love.
Anything not here, I forget it,
Anything not coming's not lost.

I live with what is and I love it,

I do not make it my enemy.
And so life has completely befriended me,
And has left me in happy simplicity."

The Immutable One

How is this even possible?
To write, perceive to feel?
Who is at the core of it?
And are they even real?

An object at the centre,
Is it really true?
Or is it based on formlessness,
Is there me and you?

Or are we one integral whole,
And the mind creates the illusion,
That we are separate people,
Subject to pain or confusion?

What is the solution?
And who is searching for one?
I give all this back,
To the Immutable one

Who isn't even one.

A Trap Made Of Tools

A person that is striving for enlightenment or God
May indeed be all part of the game.
But in an extreme it can be like a breeze
Wishing it were one with its space.

A breeze cries "I can't stop moving,
I feel separate from the stillness of air."
But the breeze's very fibre,
Is one with the air in which it appears.

The breeze is not a separate thing,
But thoughts can arise that convince it,
That it is an entirely separate thing,
That must work to get back to existence.

It is already one, 'ego' is a word,
That is only an illusory concept.
A habit may be to name all you see
When sitting in front of a sunset…

"There is a cloud, there is the sky,
There is the sun and the colours,"
Without believing in all of these labels,
There is oneness without concept of oneness.

The spiritual teachings about 'the ego',
Help expose the illusory fool.
But believing ego is a *real* thing,
Is a trap that's made out of tools.

Once you see that ego is a word,
Describing something without form.
Then the obsession of trying to get rid of it,
Is no longer the background or norm.

If you feel you must get rid of something,
It stands up and looks much bigger.
It makes you feel you are not already,
The fibre-less fibre of Nature.

Ego, literally means "I",
In this case the "I" that arises,
In the mind of a human that identifies with
All of its opinions, desires and definements.

Definements isn't a word, but you know what I mean -
Definitions and ideas of self.
Struggle no more, no one is left,
To even receive spiritual help.

Perfection Expectation

The expectation of perfection is a terrible disease,
One that leaves you carrying a mind that never feels at ease.

It creates the feeling that for you to ever be at peace,
Then the 'other' must be perfect, so be perfect if you please.

Expecting others to be perfect is a terrible affliction,
One that keep you feeling an addiction to resistance.

It is a disease I've suffered with and still do from time to time,
And I'm sorry to all those who have been subject to my mind.

I'm sorry to my mum Lorraine and I'm sorry to my brother,
If my perfection-obsessed mind has increased your discomfort.

And if I used to mock my dad for not being the perfect person,
Then I apologise and hope that I did not create a burden.

Just take it as my craziness and not to do with you,
The obsession with perfection will not give one any room.

The perfect person is not one that actually exists,
Since flaws and gifts depend only on who has interpreted.

Really they are just inventions of the human mind,
Your dog would never see you as imperfectly defined.

The expectation of perfection can start with yourself,
Expecting a perfect self can take away your health.

Always stuck in trying to be how you think you should
be,
Which may have also been learnt from before you'd
even speak.

The expectation of perfection is no longer what I need,
And gratefully the world and its inhabitants are released.

Perfect Place

Expect the world to be a perfect place,
A hostile hostage you will feel.
Allow the imperfect nature of the world,
And perfection is revealed.

Amongst the imperfect play
Of forms that we can see,
Then "right there in the imperfection
Is perfect reality."

The quotation marks signify words
By Shunryu Suzuki,
A Zen Buddhist monk who taught and spoke
On the nature of inner peace.

The Negative

One thing about being negative,
That it might not hurt to say -
That if you believe it helps you,
Then negativity may stay.

Does worrying about something
Make it go away?
Does worrying about losing something,
Make it want to stay?

Is negativity a futile act?
This is an open question.
Do you think you need it to
Prevent the bad or learn your lessons?

It is quite normal to think so,
It is the human condition,
To magnify self-punishment
And increase self-conviction.

And the negative mentality
Passes down the generations,
Where people teach each other
That negativity will save them.

Does worrying about money, create more of it?
Does worrying about tomorrow sort it out?
Is it simply an insane habit,
That we worship as if devout?

The moment you condemn yourself
Or another for negativity,
You support the very energy
That you are trying to forget.

Try to destroy it, or call it bad,
Then anything dark or negative,
Puts your energy on its back,
And infiltrates your head.

If you see as it moves, however,
That it's a futile act,
That it does not help you or your life
Become better at this or that,

Then off it drops without you trying,
It is no longer seen as real.
No longer seen as serious,
No longer has the same appeal.

But without condemnation,
Without trying to escape it,
Without ideas or judgements,
Of how it should be or how to make it,

No longer a problem to fix,
Or something to steal belief,
The old negative dictator,
Is no longer commanding chief.

Leaving Nature Clear

Negativity is only so,
When you give it a name.
In itself its energy
Is neutral, like a wave.

Call it something, it solidifies,
It becomes bigger in your life.
Don't call it good or bad,
Allow mystery, undefined.

When does positive become negative?
Where is the tipping point?
Language is our illusion,
Which can only ever point.

Don't fight the bad or try to rid
Yourself from pain or fear.
Welcome it all as the will of Life,
And they may disappear.

Or you may disappear,
Leaving Nature clear.
No more role to play,
Of resisting what is here.

The Effort of Replacement

Trying to replace negative thoughts with positive ones,
May leave you in a mess.
Attempting to fix your mind and life,
You may well try your best,

To rid yourself of darkness,
And trying to suggest,
That swapping negative with positive,
Will leave you feeling blessed.

An alternative suggestion,
Is treat them both the same.
The useless negativity,
May at first feel insane.

Without inner resistance,
Without trying to fix,
Whilst letting a voice inside
Talk as it will wish.

You may even smile at it,
It may even throw a fit,
When you no longer take it seriously,
It may seem to not like it.

And gradually it will settle,
Balance will be restored,
Where old and useless thoughts,
Will seem to walk out of your door.

When you no longer entertain a visit,
They do not want to stay.
Thoughts come and speak and argue,
Then they want to go away.

But you do have not to play,
You need not get involved,
And once their truthfulness can not be sold,
They lose the seller's hold.

Fragment

Experience isn't as personal as it appears.
Thoughts, emotions, sensations may be here.
But rather than being your personal creations,
Have they already happened?

Do they arise with your consent,
Or do they flash into appearance?
Then disappear without your coherence,
Of how they came or went?

Cling to them, declare experience as your own,
Things will feel stagnant.
See it is all spontaneous,
The self is no longer a fragment.

Fear

Fear is supposed to protect,
A barrier to keep away pain and death,
Or a force that can help to prevent
Anything happening that is not for the best.

If a snake suddenly jumps out at you,
Automatically you recoil,
Or if a fight happens,
You may know strength that is not normal.

But when does fear become attractive,
Rather than a repellant?
When does it bring to you the very thing
That you wish were kept at a distance?

A jumpy dog, for instance,
Approaches two human beings.
One is fearless, one is scared,
The dog is attracted to jumpy feelings.

So the dog is more likely to jump
On the one who wants it away.
But even if it jumps on the other,
They respond in a more effective way.

The fearful one freezes, tenses up,
Completely paralysed.
But the fearless one moves fluidly,
Without the concept of time.

A swarm of bees are angry,
Two human beings are there,
One is not afraid of them,
The other human is scared.

The fear can attract the bees,
And make the person act,
In a jumpy, jerky, violent way,
So more bees come in to attack.

Fear is not as protective
As it often appears to be,
Sometimes it attracts the very thing that
You'd really hate to see.

Or it protects an illusory identity,
Which has no real importance,
And strangles someone or makes them feel
Small and yet very important.

This is not a rule, however,
This is not condemning fear.
But rather looking at whether it serves
As well as it appears.

You may be worried for someone,
Perhaps they are out for the night.
But does projecting fear on to them
Stop them from getting in fights?
Or being hurt or anything else?
Or is it the other way round?
Do you merely create a fearful vibration,
Which can bring your energy down?

Love, however, feels protective.
If you love, you aren't afraid.
The vibration of loves dissolves your chains,
And you emanate waves that are safe.

Fear is natural in some ways,
You do not have to fight against it.
But when it becomes attached to our concepts,

It can become a foolish apprentice.

The Beauty Of Giving Up

Giving up is such a taboo,
Never, ever give up.
But when you actually look at the words,
They have a spiritual touch.

Give up. Give. Up.
Give up to something higher.
No longer rely on your own strength,
Give your task to something higher.

Give it upwards, surrender it,
Then you may well find
Far more energy to do something,
Than when you were relying on just your mind.

Love Your Ego To Death

Love your ego to death,
It is not something to be fought with,
It is not something to condemn,
It is not anything at all.

To talk about something called "ego",
Creates more illusion,
Adding to more confusion
That there is something to get rid of.

No healing occurs,
If there is a fight going on.
If manipulation is strong,
Then the manipulated keeps on.

Whatever may feel constricted,
Whatever may feel limited,
Whatever may feel painful -
Love it for no reason.

Love is the potent healer,
The powerful transformer.
Resistance create disorder,
Labels create a mess.

Love clears up the garbage,
Without even trying.
So let yourself be blessed,
And love your ego to death.

Then conflict ceases,
Struggle is depleted,
Nothing was defeated,
When ego never existed.

No need to keep playing
The ego-fighting game.
Lover and loved dissolve,
And only love remains.

Efforts

All of the spiritual efforts one can make,
Can still all be based around "me".
"Me looking, "Me meditating, "Me observing",
"Me allowing, "Me surrendering, "Me enquiring".

When the "me" is just a fake,
And it helps to sustain
Someone on the path of seeking,
Rather just putting it all to an ending,
An endless game of pain.

Contracted Seeker

The contracted seeker,
Who claims to be the speaker,
Who searches for the ether
Of his timeless self.

Is the contraction,
The personal construction,
The egoic production,
Really what you are?

Are you the one searching?
Or does the seeker arise in you?
Are you the one working?
Or does the worker arise in you?

When you sleep it all disappears, and yet in purity you remain.
Then waking comes, body appears, and you take yourself to be a name,
And a body and a mind and every single thought,
When these are only additions, to the ever-present naught.

The purity is not attached to these, making no effort to see.
But it is not something to be taken or conceived of personally.

After A Bit Of Spirituality...

After a bit of spirituality,
You may start to feel a bit rubbish.
You are told about all of the peace,
But you feel intense unease.

It's nothing at all to worry about,
Or control or try to fix.
Instead the chance to give all that up,
And no longer choose or pick.

The body and mind eject all their weight,
So it may feel intense for a bit,
Like someone who has to regurgitate,
Because inside they've been awfully sick.

Or the mind is resisting its patterns
And old paradigms being destroyed,
But in either case let it happen,
Don't judge or analyse or avoid.

Leave everything unemployed.
Then all the nonsense will stop working.
It will run out of Life to survive on,
No longer coming to you for its earnings.

"Normal"

It's weird when you look at what humans have come to call "normal".
It's normal to have desires, to not yet be quite where you want to.
It's normal to have a job that you do not like to go to.
It's normal to have problems and difficulties to go through.

It's normal for food to be sprayed with poisons and toxins,
But it's "organic" and special for food to be farmed without them.
It's normal to be struggling, to not be quite there yet,
And it's strange if you're already happy, and all your needs are met.

It's weird to have no ambition, to not want anything more.
It's strange to not have an occupation or a title to adore.
It's odd to be without a name, without identity,
With words and plans emerging from pure spontaneity.

What is natural is "strange", what is "normal" is unnatural.
Thank goodness you need not pay attention to your current human council.

A Human Weight

To believe that what happens in the world,
How people act, what they do,
What you gain and what you lose,
How you act and how you move…

…Is all completely up to you…

When you don't even know
If you'll be alive tomorrow,
Or how you came to experience the world
Or when there will be another joy or sorrow,

Is like a baby being born who says:
"What happens is up to me,
I must keep my guard up just in case
Life leaves me on my knees."
Such arrogance it seems, for a little human being,
Believing it must bear the weight of every little thing,
And take it all so personally,
Overlooking who or what it is
That causes you to see.

That allows you to even breathe.

<u>Keep</u>

Who told you that you should cling to what's already disappeared?
An event gone by, something said, perceived through eye or ear,
or nose or touch or whatever it is, it has likely passed you by,
but something inside keeps out of the light and wants to keep a fight alive,
or simply cling to what is now nothing but a thought,
why should we keep what's gone, what truly is no more?

Empty out your stores of all that's gone, the experience of Life,
don't believe you need to keep what is not even in sight.

Him

The moment we speak of him,
We cover him.
The moment we analyse him,
We no longer understand.

He is us, we are him,
Give your burdens all to him,
He is formless like the wind,
He doesn't judge you for your "sins".

And "sins" aren't even "bad",
"Sin" means "to miss the mark",
Like an arrow that does not land
On the target or its mark.

Even mind and ego,
All belongs to him.
Ego, pain, all the rest,
All arise in him.

Give it back to him.
You never even had it.
But imagining you do,
Is a painful habit.

Without him, no action,
No thought, no word, no deed,
Let him bear the burden,
Of all your Life and needs.

He will use you as he wishes,
Be silent, quiet, trust,
To a heart and mind he draws to him,
Union is a must.

He never leaves but he can show
you what it's like to wear an ego.
To feel as if you leave him,
And your own strength can mask his free flow.

Talk to him he answers,
In ways you can't predict.
Through silence, word, or influence,
Urges, people or a movie pic.

Or something you may read,
Or something you may hear.
He is already working through you my dear,
Give him all your fear.

And everything else, give him your joy,
The body belongs to him,
The mind does too, and freedom too -
All belongs to him.

He is already with you,
He is already here.
Hand him all the reigns of life,
No longer try to steer.

Your individuality
is just a game he plays.
Death proposes no danger,
And he completely takes your place.

But all this is just one way,
Of describing all of it.
If it resonates with you,
Then invite him while you sit,

Or stand or walk or talk or do,
Any which way you may be moved.

Without him none of this would be,
Give him your suffering, and you will see,

That he is both you and me.
His existence need not be proved.

The Fight

Fighting to achieve the perfect experience,
You step into the ring with a seasoned fighter.
He sticks and moves, kicks and grabs,
Two bodies entangled in desire.

Desire to control and seek,
Desire to be free,
Desire to overcome him,
And stay up on your feet,

So that you can then be free,
From a fight that steals your peace,
So that from the grip of hurt and pain,
You can finally be released.

But your opponent is so experienced,
He completely owns the ring,
And eventually even when you try,
You can not even flee.

You grab the towel from your trainer
And throw it in yourself,
Winning the fight is not worth
Any more of this awful hell.

The towel lands on your opponent's face,
The fighter can no longer see
His victim to grab on to,
To wrestle to defeat.

And while he is blinded,
You move quickly on your feet,
Merge back in with the audience,
And gently take a seat.

Seems like cowardice to many,
So many do not try,
They would rather fight all day,
Than end conflict with their life.

And although so many people
Will still fight with fist and feet,
When you make your mind the enemy,
He will never admit defeat.

It is only when you give up
From using personal might,
That comically he loses power,
Without you, there is no fight.

The Party Of The Wise

Nisargadatta Maharaj, Ramana Maharshi,
Jesus Christ and Buddha,
All invited to the party.
Papaji, Mooji, Adyashanti,
Eckhart Tolle, Byron Katie,
Krishna is already dancing.

He'll supply the music too unless there are any other
takers,
Alan Watts could even power one of the music players.
Deepak will dance to the track that signals him to move,
And Hakuin will probably bring all the party food.

And Siddarameshwar Maharaj will probably invite
Shiva,
Who may turn up the vibes so we can all turn into ether.
And I'm just sitting watching as the party of the wise
Come together to enjoy the joy and magic dance of Life.

Seng Tsan perhaps might be sitting in the corner,
And Osho might be calling for another pizza order.
And Ramakrishna will certainly be drunk with divine
love,
Whilst Mooji's cooking us some food with God's
protective gloves.

Ramana is outside and he's talking to the doves,
And Papaji is laughing as they fly from up above.
And Gangaji and Eckhart are preparing all the drinks,
While Adya is watching all the ice cubes as they sink.

And Byron is in conversation with a master with no
name,
She's talking to herself and it appears she's gone insane.
Many more are yet to come along to the party of the

wise,
Bring ignorance and Nisargadatta will destroy you with
his eyes.

Anandamayi Ma has said that that she is already
arriving,
J. Krishnamurti's with her, he says she's high, so he is
driving.
And Lama Guenden Rinpoche will come with the Dalai
Lama,
I'm going to ask Jesus if he can have a quick word with
the Father,
And multiply the presents that I am holding for these
people,
I'm holding five things, now I've got enough for fifty
people.
He says I can have more I just have to let him know,
How many more of the wise will arrive, I do not yet
know.

I will ask the Buddha, with his radiating glow,
Although to all my other queries, he says he does not
know.

I ask him and an emptiness seems to shine out from his
mind,
And he looks at me with a third eye and then quietly
replies,
(Using a gleaming body that seems merely a disguise),
That no person ever will attend, the party of the wise.

Forevermore

In a room that contains Rumi, plus guests who do not confuse me,
All is flowing very smoothly, Kabir is knocking at my door.
He asks if he may enter and as he does there is the splendour
Of a beam of light that shines from him and out into the floor.

So in the Self that's shining, all dinner guests are dining,
Divining but not dividing as they help themselves to more,
Of the source of food sustaining all the games that they are playing,
With an absence of complaining, all my guests I do adore.

And what is it they're eating but the light that shines so sweetly,
It is the light that Kabir and Rumi seem keen and hungry to explore.
The very same light, and nothing more.

And it shines, forevermore.

And as the light grows stronger now reacting to their hunger, does it engulf all of my guests who are now sitting on my floor.
And all the room goes silent, I've never known guests be so quiet, and all including Rumi and Kabir are disappearing from the dining hall.
I see the two remaining who no longer seem so straining to touch the light that endlessly pours out from beneath the centre floor.
The light fills the room with ease and then I see my

guests so pleased as the heavenly disease is wiped out from their minds and mental stores.

They are gone, and my light is shining, forevermore.

And the personal minds that seemed to shield them from the divine release, a self made of memories is dissolved in me and exists no more.

And I Am, forevermore.

Until even my light goes out, still I remain but with no shout, no sense of self impeaches on my perfection they adore.

We are. It is. Forevermore.

A Tree Did Answer Me

One day I walked up to a tree
And asked it what's the time.
It did not answer me,
And this I did not mind.

The people said to me
There was a simple explanation:
That trees have not the mouths to speak,
Or ears to hear my question.

But somewhere deep inside me,
I felt the tree did answer me.
His silence that beamed out of him,
Showed me the timelessness he sees.

And that time exists in humans,
In the minds of you and me.
And Nature moves in the stillness,
In which time does not entreat.

The trees may grow or wood may rot,
The flowers bloom and fade,
But in finding the realness of time,
No progress I have made.

Where is this supposed past?
Where can I find my future?
The tree tells me without a word,
The nature of illusion.

"Do not be under confusion,"
He says, in his beaming light,
"Although you have your memories,
Your past you cannot find.

"And the future is nothing more,
Than just a made up myth.
Based on all the memories,
Of desire, fear and wish.

"Forget the human way
Of always living in the mind,
Which is not separate from the weight
Of psychological time.

"Nature is intelligent,
Already she does fine,"
The tree has yet to say a word
But points out the divine.

I thank the tree and go home to tell
The others what the tree has said.
They suggest I visit the hospital,
In case I've bumped my head.

Our Sky

A dark cloud moves across the vast and empty sky,
Later on it passes after raining for some time.
For a while the sky is clear and it looks a crystal blue,
Then later on fluffy clouds come to make their own way through.

And while all of this goes on, whether there are clouds or not,
The sky is completely unperturbed, and it is troubled not.
What is the secret of the sky, to his inherent freedom?
He does not identify with clouds, and he does not try to steer them.

He naturally lets them come and go as if he has no power,
And so he becomes the very Life that gives Life to trees and flowers.
He does not take the clouds as if they are his personal creations,
He does not feel responsible like he must protect or save them.

And neither does he reject them, he treats a storm as he does no clouds,
All are the same for the sky, and he teaches us of how
Our nature is also sky-like, already pure and free,
And the clouds that appear in us, include the personality.

He fights with none, his very nature, is already to allow,
He does so without effort, and because of him we have the clouds.
And without the clouds we would not have the abundance of our water.
It is all nature's cycle, and the sky facilitates the order.

And neither are the clouds separate from him,
He remains throughout them, and they are carried by the wind,
That is also one with him and so he makes no separations
Between him, himself, a cloud, or all of the other great creations.

The sky is not even a personal or an individual to say,
"That I am free and allow the clouds in every single way,"
He is so free that even he is not aware of himself,
A skyless sky that is, reflects the truth of our selfless Self.

I Thank The Lord

I give thanks for the Lord, for his wisdom,
Of showing me he is in charge,
That he is not a stingy ignorer,
But a Father who loves his child.

And when he pulls you towards him,
It can first feel like a battle,
But the quicker you give up to him,
The easier it will happen.

But nothing happens really, just seeing what's a dream,
What was real and what was not, and the divinity that is free,
That cares for all things and has its own inscrutable wisdom,
Of which the intellect of the human can not even produce description.

So I give thanks to you Lord, for everything,
My family, my life, my entire situation,
The money and the comfort, the sickness and the ills,
And the peace that I feel from you in charge of all my deals.

And after reading this a few months later, now I start to feel,
That none of it was ever mine, but yours to do with as you will.

The Art Of Life

In a world promoting discontent,
To keep you chasing the wind,
To keep you buying more and stuck,
In fear of what life might bring.

Instead the wise one settles,
While his life goes singing on.
No longer struggling to get to
The next note in his song.

Not waiting for the end to come,
Not wishing he were at the start,
Life sings through him and he dissolves,
So all that remains, is art.

But with no one taking part.

Tales

The many tales we can hear
Of instant spiritual experiences,
Explosions, transcendence, wondrous tales,
Can sometimes produce interferences.

It can subtly create in the mind of a seeker
An expectation they feel they must meet,
To experience something in particular,
So they can finally feel they are free.

But this is more mind, creating ideals,
Imagining an ideal experience,
Telling you there is more to achieve,
Before you can lose all your ignorance.

These are all lies, harmlessly fun,
Like a child that's making up stories.
It's only taking the mind as worthy of trust,
That makes someone feel stuck in their searching.

Searching is taught as if it is natural,
Always looking for your completion.
Completion is here, already you are,
But searching makes you feel like you leave it.

The searching sensation then creates the seeker,
Believing liberation lies in the future,
As an experience taking you deeper,
Or an explosion leaving you fearless.

But it can happen that the mind can melt,
Over what seems like a period of time,
Like something you may cook over the fire,
Or something in the pan you may fry.

And at a certain point it is useful,
To give up the spiritual "try",
Trying to create the God inside,
When he already houses your mind.

So give up all of the expectations,
The striving and the struggle,
The searching and the mental generations,
And leave God to take all your trouble.

Everything Shines

Everything shines with the light of God,
When you no longer imagine what the world is.
When you have no idea what this thing called a world is,
Everything seems suddenly perfect.

When a mind isn't demanding it get something else,
When the rebellion against form isn't there,
Then without your intention, freedom is revealed,
And an intelligence always takes care.

A unified whole, split into fragments
By imagination and memory.
A camera-like mind takes snap-shots,
Distorting a single reality.

Then reality seems to be separate moments,
One moment after the other.
But without the addition of the camera-like mind,
It is no longer imposed by the shutter.

Joke

It's now become a joke to me
That I can't stop writing poetry,
It's bursting out my ears and now
It's spilling on the floor.

How long will this go on? We'll see,
Moved by spirit that urges me
To keep on writing till I'm sure
That I can write no more.

And then after a few hour's sleep,
I'm back awake and on my feet,
Not even remembering to eat,
Whilst this poetry I adore
Flows out from inside me
And dictates all the writing
The writer I can't find him,
Am I just a puppet
With Life as his support?

"Aren't we all?" I say as I,
Feel this poem ending's nigh,
And what the last line will be
I have no predictions for.

<u>Words</u>

Don't take words so seriously, then you are free!

No more brooding over concepts.

A simple truth that's too easy,

For a mind that wants everything complex.

Heavenly Booze

The heavenly booze
is there when you no longer wish to pick and choose,
but still, are open and in tune
to the supreme bartender.

Who decides when you can drink the booze,
like a bee that drowns in nectar,
but without the regurgitation
required for honey preparation.

All the bartender wishes to see,
is that you no longer attempt to wriggle free
from the emptiness's grip that is no longer up to you.

That you no longer move,
no longer try to escape and free
yourself from the constant embrace of she,
which is often referred to as a "he"
who's running the whole thing.

To whom the drunkards sing,
as they wonder down his streets,
completely lost in peace,
after getting drunk on heavenly booze.

Overdrink, they'll call you crazy,
perhaps overactive, or very lazy,
creative or just extremely,
Quiet and aloof…

Many other things can happen
after developing a drinking pattern,
that may not fit in with what
your friends and family approve.

But you can ignore the voices
that dissuade you from your choices,
when you find eternal freedom
sitting quiet at the bottom
of the bottle of your truth.

And strangely the empty bar
that serves the heavenly booze,
is not visited by many,
but just the occasional few.

To approach it,
no qualifications are asked of you,
but it's usually when the barman
has called you to come through.

And you may sit and enjoy the pureness
of the heavenly booze.
And when others see how great it is
they may come and join you.
The drink that leaves you
with no hangover or flu.
But a pain if you ever believe
that the bartender leaves you.

He is always there but may not always be handing out
the booze,
and why this is in absolute
truth I have no clue.

Hear the drunkards singing as they praise him in the
night,
The supreme bartender is serving their delight.

Their praises might be loud and clear,
or they might be rather quiet.
One of the highest ways to praise him,

is to worship him in silence.

And when you are with him,
You feel you can not lose.
He controls your moves,
And you, he gradually dilutes.

Oh yes he does dilute you, in his heavenly booze,
Until you are no more, and his empty bar resumes.

Gone Now

Gone now, like when you see that one drunk at the party
Who's had too much to drink and now he's lying on the floor,
And now he's back up again and wandering around,
And the people all try to stop him from drinking any more.

And he ignores them and takes a final sip of his beloved nectar,
And he loses himself so much that he wouldn't recognise his own passport.
No more fight left in him to remember battles fought,
And he dies there in the air, while suspended by the Lord.

They take him to the morgue and they cry at his demise,
When what remains in his absence, is the unspeakable divine.

The Armchair Of Being

Recline back on to the armchair of being,
Where no one is moving and no one is seeking,
No one is trying to be always achieving,
And nothing is separate from its seeing.

Recline back on to the armchair of being,
Where the freedom lies reclined.
You already are the freedom,
That you can not find.

It's just you may believe you are what feels to be a separated mind.

And the separated mind, apparently refuses to recline,
He thinks that the instructions are for him.
But the instructions aren't for him, so you need not effort to recline,
Since already you are the very being.

The very space that effort is moving in.

If something moves it moves, you need not tell a story,
Need not start a battle, or wrestle it for glory.
Instead let thoughts bore you, so that they are boring,
And an interest in the painful will certainly be falling.

And finally the armchair of being is your eternal resting place,
That can act as the hub that gives the inspiration to create,
Or simply disappear into the natural state.

Recline back on to the armchair of the being.

What Is Money?

What is money?
I don't know.

Any idea I have on it can interrupt its flow.

Or perhaps it makes no difference.

You can call it bad or good,
Call it real or an illusion.
Condemn or praise it in conclusion,
Our just get lost in a confusion.

Or it can be left alone,
Free from ideas that you may trust.
Free from fear and free from lust,
It is clear though, there is enough.

If we start to condemn money,
We may make a mistake.
When its power or effects,
Are from the human brain.

Any power money has,
It all comes from the humans,
We believe in it, or worship it,
Or label it delusion.

Feel it in abundance,
So it's bursting out our pockets,
Or be stupid so whilst people starve,
We spend billions on rockets.

We fear it, or resent it,
Or call it a collusion.
Or decide there's not enough of it,

When we hear it from the newsroom.

Perhaps we have made it so extreme
To become a necessary brother,
That if you don't have this thing called money
Then this means that you will suffer?

And is this actually a rule?
Was it learnt from father or mother?
Did you learn it from early,
Perhaps even whilst at school?
And so money can be associated from an age extremely
early,
With lack or pain, struggle and strife, or people with no
mercy.

Or money can actually be a wealth creation tool,
To create a life that's sustainable, to live life already full.

We can think that money is the wealth, but of course this
is quite funny,
Money of course creates the wealth, since by itself you
can't eat money,
Nor use it as a shelter during rain or the night-fall.
But you can use it to create a living space that's strong
and beautiful,
A home that works alongside the Earth, that happens to
be lovely.

Perhaps it's just our lack mentality that makes things
seem so painful,
And money is really innocent, but human minds make a
painful label.

Money can be used as such a beautiful tool,
But perhaps need not be given such extreme importance.
Not honed in on so completely, so that all else is

ignored,
Forgetting that the Earth is our main insurance.

If money replaces Life and Nature as what makes you
feel supported,
And people believe survival depends on a resource that's
in shortage,
Then this only creates a world similar to hell,
Where people feel abandoned and very fearful for
themselves.
So people work and toil and sweat to keep their heads
above the water,
While some billionaires in boats sail by, employing all
the paupers.

They call out from their yachts and ships, with their
direct orders,
And news that they so kindly bring directly from their
borders,
That "There's not enough", "There's a recession on", or
"There is a financial crisis",
While sitting on a pile of cash so large it's like a private
island.

Money can be wonderful when this is kept in mind:
That the truest bank is the very land that continues to
provide,
All our food, our resources and what we need to live,
And we need no longer ignore the sun for all the energy
it gives.

That to get our energy we need not dig and drill and dig.
But look to energy that's clean, that doesn't need a dirty
rig.

Renewable resources need no longer be suppressed or
hindered.

The WWF have said
that for our energy needs to be met
using solar panels, the amount of land required would be
one percent.
One percent coverage of solar panels, to supply to all of
the rest.

In a world that is commodified you may be taught it as a
fact
That you must work for everything, so shut up and pay
your tax.
But as you wake from sleep, and look up at the sun,
To what degree did the sun request a percentage of your
funds?

And when the rain falls from the sky, ask it how much it
will charge,
It will not understand you, and it will nurture all the
plants.

We are basically plants as well, with different breathing
systems,
We have different organs but of course the elements are
consistent.
When did we become so strange and commonly insane?
Making a misery out of what was only meant to be a
game?

So next time someone says that nothing is for free,
Take a breath of oxygen and put your mind at ease.
And walk away into the woods and ask all of the trees,
How much council tax they pay in order to live free.

Nature is not an evil mum who's regretting that she had
you,
But a caring loving clever force that's ready to protect
you.

A paranoid child believes indeed his parents are out to get him,
And in his mind his mother's harsh and evil, and it scares him.

If a symbiotic relationship becomes harmful to one partner,
Then the one who's being harmed, is likely to discard of the harmer.
If we continue to live like parasites instead of in harmony,
Then Nature may wipe us out, like an impermanent disease.

Or as George Carlin said, like a dog shaking off its fleas.

Is money actually something that is separate from Nature?
Perhaps it seems like this when we ignore our own creator.
And then replace our trust in Life with money as the symbol
Of a caring loving force that sustains and protects from pain and evil.

If money replaces Nature, it goes from beautiful to ugly.
And we think it is so real that it seems it can enslave us.
And people then begin to fear of not having enough money,
Since of course nobody willingly wants to be left hungry.

We've just twisted it, we've messed it up, we've asked money to do all.
We've developed strange beliefs about survival, and universal laws.

If we get confused about this thing that we call money,
And it becomes the only thing for survival that we ever use,
Then we start to have strange ideas and even stranger foolish views.
Everything turns nasty if it is terribly abused.

Food is not from money, it is not a product of the purse.
Originally it grows, organic in the Earth.
Money can be exchanged for it, but often we can forget,
That food can still exist, without paper, card or check.
And water is not a commodity that can be sold unto the people,
Since it falls from the majestic sky that covers us all equal.

I feel it is so beautiful when money is approached like this,
A tool that we can use but not abused or negative,
That if you do not have it, this does not mean you will starve,
No longer linked to suffering, or being chucked out on your arse.

That people's basic needs are met regardless of financial situation,
Can you imagine what a different world would be, if the so-called "nations",
Said actually, we are a community, we will look after each other,
We have enough to remove fear of not having the basic comforts.

That money will no longer be used to express our fear and lack,
But to express that for healthy human beings, there is enough for that.

It's not that money has to be eradicated,
But it's madness when there is enough, that people feel isolated.
That feel even being alive is a huge and massive struggle,
When the planet is abundant and provides without any trouble.

"There is enough! There is enough!" sometimes I feel to scream,
And all else including money can be built upon this theme.

Some would say that money is actually based on debt and lack,
But hopefully you get my point, and we won't go into that.

You may think all this is unrealistic but I'm not sure that it is,
If it's true that we spend over two trillion dollars on war in just a year,
But just to end world hunger, that yearly it would take,
30 billion dollars to end all people's hunger pains.

30 billion may seem a lot, but not compared to two trillion.
And in case you are not sure, a trillion is a thousand billion.
And it may not be so simple and easy as writing this,
But it is pretty bloody obvious that our mentality must shift.

I don't have all the answers, I just began to write,
And started off with no ideas, on money or on Life.
All is part of Nature, let's give her back control,

And stop acting like stupid kids leaving home at three years old.

In The Meadow

Amidst all movement, fickleness and noise,
In the meadow of bees and birds and insects and grasses
and flowers.
All flying, growing, creeping and slowing,
Flowing and weeping and possibly moaning.
The ground on which it all plays, of being, remains
untouched and untamed.
Unframed and unnamed, always unchanged,
Whilst we are out in the dancing meadow, looking for
something to remain the same.

<u>Yes</u>

How many more poems do you want to make tonight?
I'm feeling very tired now, and it's clearly late at night,
Or early in the morning perhaps would be more precise.

But let me make no mistake, I am grateful,
To be a tool to use, and hit me with your views,
What would you like to put down on this paper?

That every effort made to realise truth,
Is an effort that takes place, in the ever present you.

It Started With Cake

"If you eat that cake, it will just add to your waist",
A statement such as this seems to be a serious mistake,
Which keeps you buying diet products and going to the gym,
The shop is selling you cake while their magazines say you should be thin.

If all you ate was cake, then perhaps that would be no good,
But following what you hear on food can influence your mood,
And it can help, but it can make you focus on all the things you do not want,
Like illness, disease, fatness and size, and when you put that focus on,
Then you will just attract the things that you are negatively holding.
In your mind do not hold the things you do not want to be owning.
Instead eat well for your health, not because bad things will make you fat,
Ingest goodness out of love, rather than trying to avoid a painful trap.

Don't approach the body whilst even thinking of disease,
Treat it with completely the opposite mentality,
That care can be taken and you may eat certain things,
Because the body is healthy and it thrives in love and ease.

No need to brush your teeth to stop getting cavities,
But because you love the teeth that allow you to easily eat,
See the difference that there is in vibration and frequency,

Which is the source of your life, results and action it will breed.

And then you are more in touch with it, not blindly following
The next fad or phase or scam or trick that may be emerging.
And all the useful information can serve you on your journey,
And the intelligence of the body tells for what it is hungry or is thirsty.

Jokers

Jokers they come, telling jokes disguised as lies disguised as truth,
Many always pretending to be you.
And it is always funny when they are suddenly exposed,
As jokers who are trying to entertain you.

Thoughts dance like performers, who entertain the king,
Hopefully the king is not addicted,
To needing and believing that he must get entertainment,
From every single joker in the kingdom.

With his belief they dance and tell him jokes,
His constant interest will sustain them.
And if he believes that their little jokes are true,
Then he begins to feel drowned in a kind of madness pool.

All these jokers, jesting around him,
Trying to convince him of their words,
Then suddenly he laughs again,
Back on his throne he's perched,
As he realises that believing all of these
Crazy little words,
That were intended to be jokes,
Was absurd.

Human Advice

Look around at what humans have made,
We have been a bunch of idiots.
Technological advancements, inventions of course,
But still full of conflict and misery.

And scarcity, and fear, and alienation,
And isolations and discrimination, and segregation,
And poverty and equality and all the rest,
So beware of a human's advice for living.

Including this advice as well,
How much can you trust a human?
Particularly if they are just parroting
Simply what others have taught them.

Outside voices can sometimes help,
But the best ones seem to be
The ones that point back to the source of your self,
Where wisdom lives for free.

The being within, intelligence itself,
Spontaneous with intuition,
Which can flow into the heart and guide you,
Without depending on outside tuition.

Someone may teach you how to plant a tree,
And how very beautiful this can be.
And with practical knowledge now in the mind,
The wisdom can merge out from within.

Practical knowledge from the past,
Like how to speak a language,
Can be influenced by the inner guide,
To create something new and fantastic.
But if you take humans too seriously,

If you believe in all their names and labels,
Your world becomes purely conceptual,
Covering reality in fables.

A dream world emerges, purely of thought,
Which claims to represent your life.
And usually the world that gets passed down
Involves a past of struggle and strife.

Your name came from somebody else,
It was not attached to the body.
What you are like, who you are,
Has come mainly from other voices.

The guide is within, the universe itself,
Which projects itself out as the world.
Let it move out, it lives in the heart,
And it can influence things very well.

Salvation On A Screen

Salvation on a screen,
Or perhaps in a movie,
On a laptop or your TV,
Worshipping the screens.

They tell us what to do,
Like they are glowing gurus,
Attracting pure attention
Without any hesitation.

Three eyes all so strained,
But without complaint,
Since temporarily the screens
Can put our minds at ease.

Masking mind's discomfort
From moving relentlessly,
And instead becoming one with
Whatever's on the screen.

The pixels are supreme,
Millions of Godly light beams
Telling us what to think.
There's a reason why they named it
Television Programming,
Programming the one who sees.

Think as the screen portrays.
Whether it's about all our mistakes,
Or something that you're told is great,
Just follow all the screen will say.

Lack and fear tend to cover up
The background breakthrough stories,
That point out that in fact we live

On a planet that is supportive.

Keep the screen on night or day
To avoid all of the noise,
That has been stored up over the years
In a warehouse that covers joy,

To prevent that inner critic
That simply feels like pain,
From all the things it will say,
The screen offers to save.

And if you turn it off,
Your mind may bite you from above,
As it hungrily surveys,
The place for a thing to love.

It is all a distraction
From the infinite interaction,
When a tiny dense contraction
Merges back into its source.

Not something that need be forced,
But at first discomfort may arise,
When you no longer seek to compromise
With an unruly restless mind.

Let it do its thing,
If it contorts and screams,
It happens when you drop your chains,
No longer acting as a slave
To everything the TV screens
Have been teaching you to think.

It's not all bad however,
There are movies that are awesome,
There are websites that will broaden

And enrich all of our lives.

And TV can inform,
It can very well serve us, it's not completely bogus,
It only tends to own us
When we use it as a painkiller, for boredom.

Humans

Humans can get a bad rap, and in these poems too,
Their madness is so easily highlighted and accused,
So that a big pile of humanity's flaws we can accrue,
And perhaps we subtly wish to create a further sense of
'me verses you'.

Do you ever wonder, if the world was completely free,
Completely at peace and remarkably at ease,
That humans would no longer be able to fuel misery
with problems,
Do we really want a world where there is no more
rebelling against dogma?

Would it be too boring when the human condition
Depends on great resistance and addiction to affliction?
Perhaps our love for conflict creates the very stories
Where corrupt power sources try to rule entire countries.

But within the human being, lies a power and a
greatness,
From where entire worlds and new dimensions are
created,
A power that is so fine and pure it can transform the
place,
Where we are no longer so obsessed with the next thing
we can chase.

Before

Before even a word is said,
Before any sentence is read,
Before the ideas of alive or dead,

You are already here.

Before you try to work it out,
Before the mind goes in or out,
Before hearing what enlightenment's about,

You are already here.

Before you give yourself an image,
Before a life becomes envisaged,
Before someone starts a pilgrimage,

You are already here.

Before your name, before your birth,
Before your body, before the Earth,
Before a spiritual word is heard,

Already, you are here.

Collapse back into God, my dear,
When you disappear, so will fear,
He may feel distant but he is ever so near,
In fact there is no distance.

Only that made of resistance,
Where the person feels like a hindrance,
To get the holy deliverance.
But even ego is made of God, and belongs to the great
existence.

My Thinking Hat

Lost in a deep dark forest I search for my way out,
But I stumble and I hurt myself as I step and tread about.
I whisper and I call, and I yell out and I shout,
But I still seem to be lost in an inevitable forest ground.

Who will come to save me? Will they even notice
That I have left from home without return?
I wonder when my rescue party will eventually arrive,
And if they've even sent out people who can do a
search?

The more I try, the more I struggle,
The more I become entangled.
My thoughts all tie me up in knots,
In a spider's web I'm being strangled.

And as I dangle now in a tree so very helplessly,
Caught amongst the thorns and all the bushes,
The branches all relax as I remove my Thinking Hat,
And as I empty out my mind, I walk out with ease.

The trees leave me in a peace,
They yield, and bow down to my knees,
As a simple route for myself is made so clear.

I can barely speak,
But I feel very strong indeed,
No longer weak and I can feel
The solid strength beneath my knees and feet,

As I feel the Earth completely supporting me.

I walk out on the path prescribed,
Gentle walk with clear moonlight,
Illuminating my path towards my door.

And still without a thought do I
Thank the night and thank my life,
For releasing me from the trees alive,
Or perhaps from releasing me from my many incessant
thoughts.

And the forest and the night
Seems to quietly reply,
As if almost shy,
But with an ever-present Life, that says:

"Of course."

And so the next time I will leave my home,
To go out on the land and village to roam,
I will not bother to wear my usual clothes,
And instead I will leave my Thinking Hat, at home.

…But I will remember trousers.

<u>Animals</u>

Animals can teach the art of how to take a life of things,
The flow of life and the movements, and not interpreting,
Not commenting on everything that apparently does happen,
And not internally complaining after all their interactions.

If you by accident wake a dog up very early in the morning,
Perhaps while it is dreaming or perhaps while it is snoring,
It does not resent or curse you for disturbing it from sleep,
And in its mind and memory, the wake-up it will not keep.

So when you see it later it will not be carrying in its head -
That because of you it was disturbed from resting in its bed.
They take life as it comes, not worried for the drama,
Unless their human trainer has not known how to look after
The dog or other animal that they may wish to keep,
Never learning how to care or even train or hold a leash.
But I digress and now I'm just complaining about humans,
When the very point was that animals are not prone to great confusions,
Because they do not analyse or take things personally,
An animal can show you, the art of living free.

Even more so with animals that are not exposed to humans,

That are not infected by a mind that's full of great delusions.
A bird that flies and sings, or a spider on its web,
One with their surroundings, not stuck in their heads.

So watch an animal that you may see, and notice its freedom,
The spirit dances through it, creates and sustains its own existence.
The light that shines behind it that is not quite of this world.
But without it we would not even see a bird or read a word.

Perfect Person

Life makes no perfect person,
So we need not bear the burden
Of trying to perfect a mind that's inherently flawed.

That despite our good and bad side,
We can not sit back in de-light
Until we are broken by the light
That is our very source.

If we all had perfect thinking minds,
Then we would have no reason why
To get back to and try to find
The power that brings us forth.

And when we no longer seek it
As an object or experience,
It is evidently surrounding us
And flowing through our very core.

Then nothing is seen as separate,
Even a mind that feels hesitant,
Or perhaps is upset at the state of affairs
Of theirs, or of yours.

So now that no one's perfect,
We can no longer try to own it -
The fact that we or others should be
The perfect persons to adore.

Perfection lies, without a cause.

A Conversation With The Earth

One day I had a conversation with the mighty Earth,
She said:

"These humans for me are only surface hurts.
They do cause me some trouble, but deeply at my core
I'm ok, and I'm healthy, of that you can be sure.
Although on the surface I can not take much more
Of people treating me as if I were a nuisance,
Something to just get out the way or something to cover
and spray,
Or something that is a controllable confusion.
Almost like I'm out to get them and if they are not
careful,
Then they'll receive a dark and desolate place.
Maybe that will happen if they carry on like madmen,
Sucking me dry and leaving me barren from day to day.
You have no idea what all this is capable of,
It is not just some fantasy, that there's a possibility
That people need not have a load of pointless dreary
jobs,
But instead work hand in hand with Nature, who
provides a lot.
And nature takes care of their needs without them even
needing to plead,
If humans would only see, that all of their individuality
Is an energetic and thinking-based illusion."

"When will that happen?" I said,
"Already it has," she said, so let it be,
And be done with all of the terrible and bad news.
Hold the frequency of truth, and cease to hold societal
views.

Meditation

Meditation is not for the person,
In meditation the person is dissolved,
Or at least it is seen as merely fickleness of being,
A movement that has no real reality at all.

But if the energy you are believing
In the head that seems to be speaking
To be you,
Then you may end up feeling all caught up in it all,
When you are that in which all of it already unfolds.

Meditating as a person to achieve a certain thing,
To get somewhere or feel a certain way,
Is like a leaf that lands in the middle of a lake,
And starts to say what direction it would like the
currents to now take.

If you sit and you dictate, but not give yourself away,
Then you might feel like a solid ball of stress,
That lives and breathes energetically somewhere in the
head,
And won't shut up all day, or when you are in bed.

A personal energy always wants something,
It is programmed to feel restlessness and lack.
And so even in meditation it hunts for celebration,

Just do nothing.

Who is the instruction for?

A Spiritual Diagram

If I drew I diagram for some spiritual instruction,
A diagram to illustrate a point,
Then whatever I would draw, a body or a mind,
Something to show emotions and something to show
thoughts;

Even a personality who struggles with mentality,
Who can resist or can accept or can't do anything at all.
Then all the while I'm pointing or I'm drawing or I'm
speaking,
You are the entire paper, on which the diagram is drawn.

Which Are You?

A movement and shadow on a mansion of stillness
that does not want to be stuck and unable to move.
And death scares it, it feels chained down and struggles
to not be stuck in stillness like it's glue.

But which are you? Are you the one that moves,
The character that suffers day to day?
The one that is afraid to lie in the stillness without
movement,
And let it swallow them up, or carry them away?
Or are you the ever free, background of this illusion?

Heavenly Applause

If a sense of spiritual struggle does arise,
There is perhaps only one thing I can advise.
That understanding anything with a superficial mind,
Is like dropping a drop of water in a mine,
And then deciding the drop of water, you must find.

Give it up, don't rely on your person,
The personal mind or the individual strength.
Give it to the source, the Lord, who is really quite a gent,
Or quite a lady, who takes the burden from your head.

A word need not be said, the holy presence lives,
And breathes and experiences "you".
When you are trained to be the sole source of your
individual strength,
It may take a while to readjust, and surrender it to truth.

An ego can quickly jump up and take up a new burden
"Of discovering myself" or "finding God",
And maybe God laughs at this impostor that he made,
Who in God decides that he must do God's work.

If you as a person, a separated self,
Disappear and reappear after sleep,
Then how ridiculous it seems, to truly believe
That on you is the spiritual responsibility.

The burden is the Lord's, stop trying to steal it,
And instantly, the heavens they applaud.

And this is not just limited to spiritual endeavours,
But all the deeds of Life, which he supports.

What Fun

Something so sacred and uninvasive,
Is intimately you, but not interested in your life.
It is not counting you merits, your successes or your failures,
And in it you may curse, praise and even say your prayers.

The house of all which is so uninterested
In interfering with anything that is seen.
That it stands alone and unconcerned and yet simultaneously,
Is one with all that it can see.

Eyeless, mouthless, without any kind of shape,
Without even a sense of presence that arises,

The original nothingness which is the basis,
This marvelous existence it comprises.

The ever-free nothingness which is not what the mind will think,
It is not the nothing you may imagine.
Not a blank space you stare into,
Not an abyss that tries to tempt you,
But so free that it is beyond the mental reach.
At yet it is not separate from the mind that thinks it sees.

Grasp it with your mind, say you understand,
Then thoughts again may be dancing and deceiving.
Notice as these words appear from the voice that says them in the mind,
That as quickly as they appear, they're disappearing.

Nothing is separate, give up all distinctions,
No need to separate consciousness form its very source,

No need to think consciousness is separate from thoughts,
Let the life dance on, like a beautiful waltz.

And as the two dance together, they are one.

What fun.

Sacredness

Sacredness in the house,
Sacredness in the land,
Sacredness in the air,
Sacredness in the hair,

Sacredness when you look but no longer call a chair "a chair",
Something that is shining, is always shining there.

Sacredness in movement,
Sacredness in thoughts,
Sacredness in devotion to the fundamental source,

And sacredness is always in the very air you breathe,
Especially if you are in an area with trees.

Sacredness in reading,
Sacredness in touch,
Is easily overlooked,
Then sacredness is lost.

But is never really lost,
Just no longer so apparent.
The sacredness of Life is not something that waits to happen.

It is there when you no longer are trying to be elsewhere,
When what the next moment may bring, is no longer your care.

And sacredness is something then naturally you share,
When the mystery of Life remains mysteriously bare.

Trapped In Stillness

Trapped in stillness there is no escape,
And my oh my how I have tried for years.
An escape that seemed so real, but now seems no big deal,
Since wherever I go, stillness just remains.

It even houses thoughts, and is inseparable from these forms,
So stillness and the forms are not kept separate.
It is not some state that exists when an absence of noise is here,
But a comforting and all the same, unescapable place.

Treasure

There is no need to go searching for treasure,
When all the riches lay within your own heart,
What keeps us from finding the source of our wealth,
Other than the belief that we have been set apart?

Wealth is presented as something distant,
Something far away to be achieved.
Wealth is already here in the richness,
Of seeing we have all that we need.

A wise man said that knowing what is enough,
Is surely the meaning of wealth,
But wealth is portrayed as far away,
And a distance away from yourself.

All the Earth's riches are the reflection of us,
The abundant and vibrant being,
That lives as the whole universe,
Not knowing what "lack" even means.

The Happiness Boat

Happiness is a boat, sitting on a lake,
And for Happiness what humans do is make a big mistake.

The boat that they are sitting in has writing on the side,
The word reads "Happiness" and it is obvious to the eye.

But they can't see the word since they are already inside,
So unknown they sit in Happiness, sitting side by side.

And when humans are in the boat, a discovery they make,
That overboard the letters are reflected in the lake.

So as they stare down at the lake, feeling so very happy,
And read "Happiness" that shimmers in the water so very gladly,

They jump out of the boat from where they comfortably sat,
And they end up in the water, landing with a splash

Then they get in trouble and they're struggling for air,
Because they can not swim well, and they were not prepared,

To land out in the water and find out they had been cheated,
By the words that the water merely reflected and repeated.

But for a while they still declare that happiness they saw,
Lurking in the waters and it's happiness they adore.

So they search and search no longer feeling happy as

before,
Since happiness was abandoned when they jumped off overboard.

Will they make it back inside the boat? Only time will tell.
Don't look now, but more are jumping overboard as well.

Perhaps they want to reach the others and offer them their help,
Happiness remains, abandoned by the little selves.

Picking Up Things

A child wanders around and picks up everything it sees, and after a few years has the ability, to place all that it sees in all of its many memory stores.

Picked up from the loving parents, or the teachers or grandparents, or those in life that mistreated you, who cared not for you at all.
Or even from the friends that you have gravitated towards.
Or from the screens of pixelated scenes, that offered to put your mind at ease, educating you in thinking even before the tender age of four.

Picking up beliefs and habits, as if they were all fluffy rabbits, until the rabbits get too heavy and you can't carry them anymore.

And then they start to bite you, you do not want to fight them, so you let them go and they release you, and they don't touch you anymore.

Things you may pick up in life, from friends, elders or parents,
That truly go unquestioned, as often as the law.

Things like worry, ideas of money, what it means to work and what it means to be a bore,
What it means to be lazy, how thick should be the gravy, or something so simple as how to give someone applause.

Some of them are helpful and can serve us very greatly,
But watch out for the many that knock on the house of madness and his door.

From inside his house they knock, shaking and shouting on the spot,
Or so quiet inside that you do not detect them sleeping on the floor.

Claiming to be normal ways, of getting by and acting sane,
Suffering and limiting yourself until your mind is sore.

Notice all the drama, pain, that from beloveds, you used to take,
As perfectly normal ways of what life should be for.

When in fact you may then see, that secretly or quietly,
They are the very epitome of madness and insanity galore.

Just the little habits, or the background sense of panic,
Or the belief that if you don't hold on, then life will drag you to the floor.

Pulling you down, and nothing more.

And when all this is noticed, it's like a bird that had a rope which had tied it down, but now it's free, and up into the air it can swiftly soar.

And when you fly through air so pure, no longer of dysfunction sure, then you can laugh at it all, and the freedom is all yours.

Returning Home To The Kingdom

A man is lost, wondering the streets,
He is looking to find his home.
He searches for years and wanders around,
He is cold, hungry and alone.

He eventually finds the palace that's his,
With a kingdom that's all for him.
He runs up to the door, the door opens up,
And a voice says, "Please come in".

And then he steps back, like a knee would jerk,
If you tapped just above the shin.
Now he was scared, and he wondered if,
He should stay outside with rain and bins.

"This is all yours," the kingdom spoke,
"Why is there so much fear?"
"Because" said the man, "if I enter this place,
I fear I may disappear.
I feel it already, my self slips away
As I step into the light of the kingdom.
Madness it would be, to give myself up,
Even if this is my dominion."

"Yes, it is home!" the voice replied,
"The place of pleasure and comfort,
And yet you decide to stay outside
Like you are waiting for a dump truck."

And while hovering around outside,
Still hovering by a bin,
An arm reaches out, grabs my mind,
And pulls me directly in.

And after pulling me in,

There is the richness of the kingdom,
Wealth and glory all around,
But no-one left to keep them.

The Party Hall

All spiritual effort, takes place in what?
Takes place in who? Could it be you?
Without an idea of "you", but existence all the same,
All that will remain, when you no longer cling to name,
When you no longer decide, that form is where you live?

The efforts to realise it, all dance within it,
Like a party hall that is filled with dancing kids,
The kids demand that they find the party hall,
And the mother of the birthday kid cries "your in it!"
But one child refuses to believe, to sit and notice quietly,
And so he goes on searching till the end of the party.

And he's annoyed that he could never find the wonderful
party hall,
That everyone had told him was fantastic.
But he leaves somewhat defiant that on his strength he
remains reliant,
That one day he may find the wonderful and allusive,
famous party hall.

He simply has not got it that while he searches for the
object both the objects and the searching arise in the
party hall.

He is merely an appearance in the timeless party hall.

And when he returns he could enjoy the play and fun,
but is all obsessed and all too glum in his endless search
for this majestic and magical party hall.

He has ideas of how it should look which means he can
not see it, since he is searching for the image that the
mind presents to him,
Of the floor and kids and colours and decorations on the

walls.

Which should produce sensations of wonderful revelations as his now huge expectation rises and does not look like it will fall.

All he wishes for is to find this famous party hall.

And all the time the party hall remains, still and completely quiet as all the children play, motionless and silent so that the child within can not see or notice it at all.

Then finally the child relinquishes his need to find the mysterious and ever allusive and ever hyped-up perfect and magical party hall.

And he notices that whilst he was searching, whilst he was crying and whilst he was yearning, all the time for what he was searching housed and watched the entire search and more.

It is evident already, ever calm and ever steady, present beyond presents already,

The beloved the party hall.

The Magic Show Of Life

Life's like one big magic show, where the magician
can't be seen.
Everything instantly disappears at the same time it is
seen.

As soon as you describe something, it has already
changed,
morphing, falling, or vanishing, before you can give it a
name.

A magic show that's dancing, just for our entertainment,
but of course the magician's tricks are kept secret from
spectators.

One of his most fascinating of all his many tricks,
is to make everything disappear as soon as we've seen it.

The past that we all think is our own has vanished from
our eyes,
and the only place it lives on is in our greedy little
minds,
which want to keep so many things - ideas, memories
and people,
so it becomes overfed and performs all sorts of evil.

It just needs a rest from consuming, from keeping,
hoarding and eating,
and yet even this same mind, is the magic show defined.

Where time and people seem to exist, when they are just
creations of thought.
Events and time as a linear thing is maintained as
truthful lore.

But when examined if in fact time is really real,

or if you can find your future, then the timeless stands revealed.

Then time is more like a sensation that swears truthfulness in mind,
but the magic of this entire thing is the emptiness of time.

The magician carries on performing with effortless grace and ease.
When we believe we are running the show, we cover up all our peace
with painful effort and straining, striving to make the show
exactly how want it to be, so after applause we can let go.

Or so we can maintain ourselves as accomplished magicians,
but as we try to perform it all, we sit in the audience's position.

Let the magician do his thing, you need not get involved,
and finally we can enjoy the show, and let it all unfold.

He may take some requests, and other times may not,
since the requests still have to fit in with his predetermined plot.

He may call up some volunteers and make them look like fools,
but even when he does this, they are his beloved tools.

If the audience forget that it's just a show for entertainment,
then they may become tense and rigid and fall victim to derangement,

and forget the show is all within the safety of his arrangements.

De-Fined

Give up your definitions, if only for a moment.
Give up the naming, labeling and avoidance of atonement.

Everything is moving, subject to great change,
But our definitions act as if all will stay the same.

If every thing is moving, never standing still,
Then definitions of static-ness can not possibly be real,
And things can not match up to a personal will.

Describe something a certain way, now it might be different,
It might have gone or grown or shrunk or never even been existent.

Defining and interpreting can enhance the sense of time,
While everything in life also does become de-fined.

The fineness of things becomes obscured by a veil of mind,
Making a load of noise out of what is silently divine.

And so now they are de-fined, things no longer shine,
And actions that are selfless become an object of our pride.

All becomes personalised, we blame and criticise
The self we think is acting out behind someone's eyes,
That decides what it does and says, and thinks and knows and feels,
When all is the totality, the walking talking field.

Carry The World

Carry the world, carry the world,
Carry the world on your head!

Appear to be born into it,
Then carry it until you are dead!

Bear all of your burden,
Worrying no end!
Depend on time and certainly,
The present do not befriend!

Otherwise you will be free,
In the pocket of existence,
Owned by an intelligence,
That is beneath human resistance,

Please remain in ignorance!
Remain in separation!
Be dominated by fear
And a lack-based mental hindrance!

Please oh please do not relieve
Yourself of a disease,
Of giving strength to the belief
That you are a separate entity.

Above all else do not see
The power of life that moves with ease,
Which has no need to be complete
Or made more full or more at peace.

Please do not abandon the
Idea of time and certainly
Maintain your fear of uncertainty,
Depend on all your concepts.

Keep feeling in a shortage,
Do not give up yourself,
It would be so bad for your health
To give Life back to Life...

To disappear in harmony,
Intuitive inspiring,
Not working or retiring,
Without a sense of stress.

So please, keep the world inside your head.
I think that would be best.

The End Of Struggle

Struggling to be something you were told to be,
Struggling to have something you think you have not.
Struggling to be someone you think you should be,
Struggling to achieve your life's lot.

Will the struggle ever end?
When you get it, or when you are it,
Will the struggling mind no longer pretend?
Pretend to be somewhere it shouldn't be?
Or will it choose something else to struggle over,
And the struggle begins over again?

Or the struggle to keep or maintain ensues,
The attachment becomes stronger than ever,
Struggling to hold on to no longer struggling,
When things change as easily as the weather.

Is the psychological struggle helpful?
Does the tension, the pain inside help?
Does it give you more energy and life-force?
Does it drain you, or does it keep you well?

Struggling is given great value.
It is presented like a badge of honor.
A pre-requisite, it seems, as something you need
To achieve what is deemed as important.

The mental struggle for this and that
Is just a load of pain.
And everyone searches for the eventual day
When this pain will no longer remain.

But the struggle can vanish, you need it no more,
To move or act in life.
The struggling mind is not currency

That buys you the achievement you'd like.

Struggling mind suffocates,
It makes unhappy, clogs things up,
But often presented as the very helper
Which will help to carry you up.

But to give up this struggle is a struggle,
When you think you know better than Life.
When situations are wrong and you are right,
And you end up in a terrible fight.

Arguing and struggling, wrestling with things,
To make them as you want them,
And so your helpful events-organiser
Is rejected and quickly forgotten.

Life is what gives you the very energy to wake,
The movement that moves and breathes,
It inspires your thoughts and calls you to act,
And does so with relative ease.

If you make the first initial effort,
Of struggling away from that,
Then you may well feel a struggle for things,
Even doing nothing can seem like a drag.

The struggle can also be addictive,
It makes you feel like a separate person.
And so no longer struggling creates resistance,
Like you'd rather keep yourself and your burdens.

There's also of course the need to achieve,
That gets dumped on your head as a kid.
If you're taught that to struggle and achieve things
Is the purpose of life, then it is.

It will feel like you are here for the reason,
To achieve something with "your" life.
When these are just words society gives
And keeps you feeling in constant strife.

If you struggle, you don't enjoy,
And enjoyment breeds success.
So enjoy, admit you know nothing,
Forget the rest, including the stress.

What Is Wrong?

A main form of human misery,
Is believing something should not be.

But holding the resistive energy,
Keeps you in that frequency.

It may be something you can see,
Behind the eyes or out the other side,
It may be how you think life is,
Compared to how it "should" be,
It may be how you have "an ego"
That you feel is an incurable disease.

It may be the cost of living,
That you think should be more free,
It may be something "gone wrong"
That should not have ever been.

Whatever it is, it is helpful to notice,
What causes most pain is the resistance,
That serves as only a hindrance,
And keeps you feeling trapped inside
A body and mind or life not fine,
That should be otherwise.
But the trouble all comes from a conditioned mind,
To always declare something's not right.

If this goes away, the condemnation of things,
Of resisting nature's experience,
Then the debt drops off, you no longer make,
Daily unhappiness payments.

And what remains with no one left
To say something that appears is wrong,
A question with no answer, a peace that remains,

187

A silence that's singing a song.

And yet an intelligence, a spacious stage,
That allows action to carry on.

Limited Opinions

What society can say is bad about your life,
Can turn out to be fantastic.
But listen to the opinions of humans,
And you may be tricked in to thinking you are lacking.

The general mindset tends to be
Foolishness posing as pride,
Or knowledge supported by lies,
Or ignorance in enlightened disguise.

The narrow-minded nature of many
Dictates to life what is good and bad,
It will also tell you why you should be happy,
And will tell you when you should be sad.

Within a situation that may be called "wrong",
Like it simply shouldn't be,
There may be within it a key,
That is hidden but can be seen,

Which opens a door to gratitude
Of what the moment brings,
A realisation that what you thought would be best,
Was not as correct as it seemed.

Moments we try so hard to avoid
Can happen anyway,
And they leave you feeling deeper, freer,
Wiser or in tune with grace.

What you may have thought would be so bad,
Ends up leaving you saved,
Or broken free from hidden pains,
With attachments no longer sustained.

This is not a blanket statement,
To discount people's hardships and pain,
But what the human mind may say is best,
Is not always what Life would say.

Natural Transactions

The word "transaction" may have now taken on a
slightly dead quality,
Since it may just be associated with money.
But transactions are completely natural,
And only one of its many forms is financial.

There are trades in services or material goods,
Exchanges in ideas, exchanges in foods,
Exchanges in friendships, between relations,
Trade-offs in the many natural places.

A bee gets the plant's nectar for food,
But pollinates other flowers in the meadows or woods.
Eating food like vegetables from the land
Can lead to an exchange in a natural way -
If we all made compost out of our waste,
The stuff that remains fertilises the place,
To allow more food to grow.

The seed of a fruit passed or dropped
Would then be a new tree sown,
Which means a new tree could grow,
So the trees can proliferate,
And give even more food which would be great,
Then more seeds get back to the soil,
And the transactions continue without any spoil,
So transactions are all around.

You get something, you give a few pounds,
or dollars or whatever you use.
But perhaps we've moved away from transactional
views,
And we think more as "take take take"...

Eat the Earth's food, then flush your "waste" down the

loo,
Into your own drinking supply.
So what could have gone back into
The land and ground to produce more food,
Becomes truly "waste" in anyone's eyes -
Something to get rid of, flush and hide,
It becomes a dirty pollutant,
That we have to chemically remove,
So that we can eventually drink the water,
That was just full of our piss and poo.

We do the same with fossil fuels,
We take then only pollute.
We see what we want and then it's removed,
And we use it to heat up our rooms,
Whilst producing a load of fumes,
A constant careless consume.

If we don't benefit Nature
In the way she benefits us,
She'll easily just get rid of us
Like she's pushing us under a bus.
A virus or something cancerous
Going on killing its host,
Whilst only concerned for its safety,
It destroys its very own home.

Madness.

Life is a unified whole,
Everything interconnects,
When one aspect begins to forget,
Then it all turns into a mess.

We treat the Earth like it's here for us,
Like it serves us to act out our lives,
But maybe we are here for the Earth,

And what happens to us, she decides.

Where is the transaction,
What do humans provide?
Are we benefitting the whole,
Or are we sucking it dry?

Transactions also occur
In our social lives -
Are you giving as well as taking?
Or is somebody else only taking,
So for you, the giver, it's energy draining?

Balance is key, the breath moves in,
For our bodies to live and breathe.
Then the breath goes out and provides a need
For the breath of our neighbouring trees.

The human being balances,
The breath is the prime example.
Let Nature bring back balance fully,
By giving up the dysfunctional cycle
Of taking, receiving, of using,
But not even being grateful
For a life of tremendous potential,
Spoiled by a mindset unnatural.

It's time we all act rational,
Stop believing the land is national,
Stop caring about what is fashionable,
And give as well as we take.

It's a reflection of our minds,
Have you noticed how thoughts just go on,
Using energy all day long,
Complaining, worrying or singing a song,
Without ever taking a break?

A consuming mind, eating Life,
Producing thoughts as waste.
Never caring of its pollution,
Creating noise in infinite space.

Then this mind focused only on take,
Treats the outer world just the same,
Uses whatever energy it can take,
To maintain and feed its own face.

Not just from the Earth, but people,
Or objects that are overlooked,
Always used as a means to an end,
Or an obstacle in the way,
All in an attempt to be safe.

Abusing natural grace,
When natural grace is the very place
That the mind can never escape.
Realising its source, it sees its mistake,

And by Nature it is replaced.

Perhaps we're reluctant to give or repay
Because we learn that we are lacking,
Always in need of the next thing
To finally fill an empty space.
But to believe this is a dis-grace,
In the most literal way.

Hopefully this imbalance is just a phase
That humans will no longer chase.
I feel to say it again,
The ending four-line phrase:

It's time we all act rational,

Stop believing the land is national.
Stop caring about what is fashionable,
And give as well as we take.

A Seller In A Shop

A man walks into a shop,
With a sack of garbage on his back.
He's looking to sell all the crap
To anyone's attention he can grab.

He walks into the first shop,
He emits an awful smell,
The air becomes denser and heavier,
And the door chimes with a bell.

"I've got this stuff to sell,"
He proclaims to the shopkeep,
"It will sell awfully well,
If you stack it on your shelves."

"What is it?" replies the shopkeeper,
Disgusted but engrossed,
Uncomfortable with this man
Who stands before himself.

"I'll show you," the seller replies,
And he tips out on the floor
Garbage, rubbish, attracting flies
That followed in from outside.

"What are you doing, don't make a mess!"
The shopkeeper is annoyed.
Giving his attention to all the mess,
He feels engulfed in noise.

And now with the buyer's attention,
The seller performs his trick,
He hypnotises the shopkeep,
And the shopkeep falls for it.

The seller says it quick:

"Now I have tipped out my produce,
You simply have to buy it.
I will receive the payment direct,
Since I have directly supplied it."

The shopkeeper complies, not at all surprised
At what he's decided to buy -
The garbage that was taken from his own
Bin that was sitting outside.

The seller then goes to the shop next door,
Brings in all the rubbish.
He makes his announcement at the counter,
But no one comes in a hurry.

He waits a while, the shop is stinking,
But still no one to buy.
After a while he loses his patience,
And he goes to the next shop to try.

And as he walks out of the door,
Leaving the shop forever,
The shopkeeper emerges at his counter,
And laughs at the seller's endeavour.

He knew that all the seller would need,
Is his precious attention of interest.
If a thought or a person comes to sell you their rubbish,
Do nothing, and there's no one to invest.

Hand In Your Resignation

Hand in your resignation
As the manager of existence,
Always keeping so many accounts
Of what's been happening and what is missing.

Deciding how things should have been
And how things should play out,
It's a twenty-four hour job,
And once you're in, you can't get out!

You may have done an ok job,
Your career may have gone quite smoothly,
But when you go to the cinema,
You don't have to control the movie.

If you sat down to watch a film,
Can you imagine the pain and unease,
If you thought that it was your job to control
All the movements that play on the screen?

Eventually the personal manager
Becomes completely tired
Of deciding how to run things,
Who to hire and who to fire.

When all the time there is another
Manager who is much higher,
Who already takes care unseen,
And does not wish to retire.

The personal one, the one called "me"
Has just been interfering with things,
Not allowing the higher manager
To get on and do his thing.

Yet the unseen manager
Still has the control.
He supports what he wants to happen
And abandons what he does not.

And he's glad to see the lower one
Hand in his resignation.
With him out of the way,
The business can be saved.

Untitled

Leave yourself untitled, like a poem unrestricted,
Free to move in any way that the writer wishes.
Not bound by words that must obey and stick with a
certain message,
Undefined and not subject to society's conditions.

The Race Against Nature

Trying to be somewhere you are not,
Hurrying to get something done,
Rushing to be somewhere else,
Is all a race against Nature.

How can you win when Nature brings everything about?

How can you get ahead of a universal moment?

Why try to drag things along when you can be carried by everything else?

If it hurts, stop racing, you can't possibly win.

Then you are carried and supported, like seeds in the wind.

God's House

I have been living in God's house,
But asleep, in my room, dreaming I have been cast out.
I have been here, in God's house,
Struggling in my dream to find my way home.

But I was dreaming.

Thank You

Thank you, thank you, thank you,
2 words that can transform.
They enhance the sweet, sweeten the bitter,
And dissolve the painful forms.

Thank you for reading, I hope you enjoyed
These poems on display.
Wonderful that the words are now gone
And the freedom beneath remains.

About Adam

There's not much to say about Adam, but you can find all of his books, meditations and free guidance at **www.InnerPeaceNow.com.**

Thank you for reading the book, I hope you enjoyed it.

If you enjoyed the book and feel moved to write a review, please do so on the book's Amazon page, or wherever you purchased the book from. It really helps the book reach more people.

Thank you.

 **@InnerPeaceNow**

 *@InnerPeaceNow1*

Also Available

If you enjoyed these poems, you may also enjoy these books by Adam:

Get Out Of The Cage: A Guide To Inner Freedom

A helpful guidebook for meditative reading with quick paragraphs for inner peace.

Happiness Is Inside:
25 Inspirational Stories For Greater Peace Of Mind

Great for kids and adults – I'm told they work very well
as bed time stories with deeper meanings.

A useful guidebook for those looking to become more
emotionally free and at ease.

An epic tale for kids and grown ups – great for sharing
deeper meanings of oneness and the power of the Earth
with the whole family.

A Tale Of Two Ninja Kids:
A Martial Arts Adventure Series

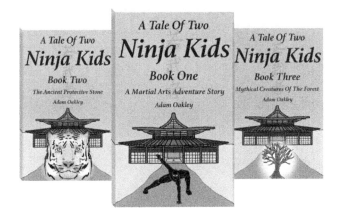

A popular children's series, these martial arts-inspired adventure books with useful life lessons for us all.

Signed and personalised copies available at
www.NinjaKidsBook.com

Follow on social media to find out more

@NinjaKidsBook

The Powers Of Ronald Berkley:
A Journey Of Awakening

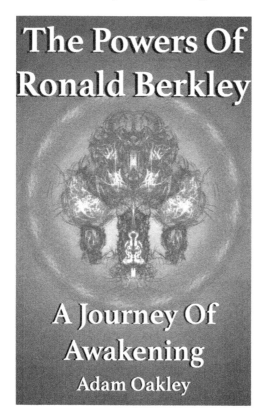

The story of one man waking up to the system that has
blinded him, and discovering his true powers when he
distances himself from those who are trying to control
him...

The Awakening Slave:
A Fighter's Story

Living as a slave forced to fight for the entertainment of others, Marxin begins to wonder if any of this is really normal...

All of Adam's books can be found on his website, InnerPeaceNow.com, and are also available on Amazon and other online retailers.

Made in the USA
Monee, IL
04 June 2020

32506079R00125